John: The Martyr's Gospel

JOHN
The Martyr's Gospel

Paul S. Minear

The Pilgrim Press
New York

The author has relied mainly on the *Revised Standard Version of the Bible* (copyright 1946, 1952 and © 1971, 1973 by the Division of Christian Education, National Council of Churches; used by permission), although in many cases the biblical quotations are translated afresh.

"John the Evangelist" by Tilman Riemenschneider, from the Munnerstäder Altar, is now in the Staatliche Museen, Berlin, West Germany. The photograph by Jörg P. Anders is copyrighted and reproduced on the cover by permission of the museum's Skulpturengalerie.

Library of Congress Cataloging in Publication Data

Minear, Paul Sevier, 1906–
    John, the martyr's gospel.

    Includes bibliographical references.
    1. Bible.   N.T.   John—Criticism, interpretation, etc.
I. Title.
BS2615.2.M53   1984   226'.506   84-7754
ISBN 0-8298-0718-7 (pbk.)

The Pilgrim Press, 132 West 31 Street, New York, New York 10001

To my Duodecim friends
who, as usual, will think otherwise

Contents

Introduction   ix

Part One:
The Character of the Conversation   1

    I. The Narrator   3
   II. The First Readers   14
  III. The Adversaries   24
  IV. The Objectives   37
   V. The Time Frame   48

Part Two:
Messages from a Victorious Martyr   57

   VI. My Peace I Give to You   59
  VII. When You Have Lifted Up the Son of
       Man . . .   70
 VIII. Ask and You Will Receive   81
   IX. If You Abide in My Word . . .   92
    X. No One Comes to the Father, but by Me   103
   XI. I Am the Resurrection   113
  XII. Where I Am, There Shall My Servant Be   123
 XIII. I Have Given Them the Glory   132
 XIV. Look! This Is Your Mother!   143
  XV. Feed My Sheep   153

Notes   163

Introduction

Although I have studied the Bible for many years, only recently have I been attracted to the Gospel of John. In fact, it has repelled me more strongly than I have been ready to admit even to myself. There must have been many reasons—subconscious as well as conscious—for this repulsion. Among the conscious reasons are several that other readers of John probably share. One of these is the dubious credibility of John's portrait of Jesus. In an age when a premium has been placed on the recovery of dependable information about Jesus, this Gospel seems far less dependable than the other three. Wherever priority is given to authentic traditions about "the historical Jesus," the value of John sinks to a low level. Even to a casual reader the portrait of Jesus is so impressionistic as to invite skepticism.

Another allergenic property is the author's recurring accent on such incredible signs as turning water into wine and raising Lazarus from the dead. John presents Jesus as a person who fully shared in the omnipotence and omniscience of God; he could do anything he desired. To an independent reader, this view borders on magic and is therefore counterproductive of the kind of faith the Evangelist appears to demand.

Still another source of resistance is the fact that John's story is so drenched with anti-Semitic prejudices that it infects credulous readers with the same poison. For centuries his tirades against the Jews have furnished weapons for fanatics to use in pogroms and holocausts. It is not strange that thoughtful people who repudiate that terrible Christian heresy should shy away from this source of infection.

For similar reasons John is far from popular with moderns who are totally committed to religious tolerance and are intolerant only of intolerance. His dogmatism seems to be absolute and absolutely exclusive: for example, "No one comes to the Father, but by me [14:6]." To such a claim a natural reaction is this: "How can we trust any writer who so flatly excludes all roads to God but his own?"

Finally, many readers find John's theological verbiage obnoxious. That verbiage has been such as to make this Gospel the favored scripture among Christians of a dubious stripe: otherworldly pietists, esoteric mystics, introspective Gnostics. The imagery and vocabulary are so vague and sentimental as to make impossible precision in thought and clear guidelines for action. The thought of John becomes an impenetrable jungle for readers who relish photographic realism, ethical practicality, or political applicability.

The more one tries to penetrate the inner recesses of John's thought, the less can one be confident of success. At every point the text confronts the reader with mysteries within mysteries, with intentional double-talk, with misunderstandings used as a literary technique, with highly charged symbols that are both allusive and elusive. Little wonder that one of the greatest biblical scholars, Adolf von Harnack, was bound to confess: "The origin of the Johannine writings is, from the standpoint of a history of literature and dogma, the most marvelous enigma which the early history of Christianity represents."[1] It is not surprising, then, that these negative features should discourage many of us from getting emotionally involved with this Gospel.

However, as a teacher, I have been obliged to introduce students to its riddles and to keep in touch with current research. The volume of that research has been expanding so rapidly that no one can keep pace with it. But in reading some recent studies I have found my admiration aroused more by the scholars than by the Gospel. In fact, some of the best studies seem to lead away from the text rather than deeper into its original orbit. In any case, my aversions to the Gospel have not been notably reduced by scholarly expositions of it.

What happens, then, when I turn from the work of scholars to the sermons of preachers? Here I must confess that most sermons based on Johannine texts reinforce the repellent features already mentioned. Some preachers trust the historical accuracy of the portrait of Jesus, indicating that two centuries of biblical science have been wasted. Some sermons use John's "spiritual" language virtually unchanged, on the assumption that it can provide ample nourishment for liberal, middle-class pieties, however superficial or synthetic. When blended with the mellifluous tones of the preacher, the sentences from the Gospel soothe anxieties, smooth over antagonisms, engender mystical dream states, and pronounce undiscriminating benedictions on any "fellowship of kindred minds." The injunctions to love are sufficiently sentimental and vague to bear endless repetition. ' Rarely is the Gospel read in church in such a way as to release the message intended by its author, who was the first preacher of these "sermons." Scholars may not be able to decipher the full meaning, but they know enough about it to cringe when they hear some uses made of the Gospel in contemporary congregations, whether by liberals or literalists, by whites or blacks, by moral minorities or moral majorities. In short, I must confess that my own allergies to John have not been alleviated by either scholars or preachers.

Recently, however, a magnetic attraction has proved to be more powerful than the repulsions. Fascination has been increasing to the degree that I have followed several simple rules: Read the Gospel; read it as a whole, over and over again; read it, insofar as possible, in its own terms as a single document; read it as a story that was first told by a particular narrator to a particular audience for particular reasons. Recall the time frame and the space frame within which the original conversation belonged. Reconstruct in imagination the human situations within which each idea derived its relevance for John. At every point try to fit your ways of thinking into John's ways, not his into yours. Free yourself from the desire to judge John by his contributions to your knowledge of the pre-Easter Jesus, and from a similar desire to judge him by the degree to which he meets your own theological or ethical predilections. Free yourself from the desire to make his teaching immediately useful in meeting urgent contemporary needs, whether personal or communal. Read as an individual who is responsible for responding to the text on your own, in terms of your own fund of talents and knowledge, rather than screening the text through secondary literature, however edifying or scientific. When a given sentence baffles, look for clarification to nearby sentences and to the patterns of John's thought. In each verse something is hidden that would surprise you, if you could find it. What you expect is *not* there; what you do not expect *is* there; look for it. Familiarity most surely, if subtly, breeds contempt of documents such as this.

As a professor, I am well aware that these rules are dangerous; they constitute a prescription for bizarre interpretations in which personal idiosyncrasies may run riot. No member of the professional guild can go off on his or her own and expect to succeed in deciphering ancient mysteries. Yet I must confess that only in following these rules has the document begun to pull my thought into new channels. And I have been unable to turn back. I hope that scholarly colleagues may forgive my lapses from academic rectitude and that my readers may share some of the surprises that have come to me as I have tried to come to terms with the author.

Among these surprises is the aptness of the title—the martyr's Gospel. The term martyr is unpopular today, and I hesitate to use it because of misleading associations. For some, a martyr is a disagreeable person who seeks sympathy by pretending to suffer or by exaggerating his or her sufferings. Such martyrs are too numerous in our day to commend their ilk. For others, a martyr is a person who accepts death willingly rather than compromise his or her faith. That comes closer to the mark, but in our day such people are too uncommon for the term to carry immediate resonance. According to a recent Gallup poll, not more than one in eight church members in America admits any readiness to make a major sacrifice for religion. Whether or not that is accurate, we all view the martyr as an exceptional person.

I use the term to call attention to four basic meanings of the Greek word cluster *martys*, of which the English word martyr is a transliteration.

1. *Martys* is a person who sees something happen and who reports to others what has been seen.
2. In the case of prophecy, a *martys* is a person who sees and hears invisible and inaudible things and who reports to God's people what has been seen and heard.
3. In the case of legal procedures, whether actual or metaphor-

ical, a *martys* is a person who is hailed before a court and who is called on to give a testimony that will result in acquittal or conviction of criminal charges.

4. All three of the above meanings lie behind the development of a fourth: A *martys* is a person who, on trial for life, refuses to recant faith and who willingly accepts death as the price of fidelity.

The Gospel of John is a story about Jesus, in whose life and death all four of these meanings are illustrated; it is also a prophetic anticipation of the vocation of his disciples that will illustrate all four meanings. That is why John's book can be called, in technical terms, a martyrology. That is also why the verb to testify *(martureō)* and the noun testimony *(martyria)* are so prominent in this book. So I have chosen my title to underscore the fact that Jesus is the primary witness, that he required the same kind of testimony on the part of his disciples, and that the narrator of the Gospel, whom for convenience I call John, accepted the same role for himself.

To say more than this about the title would be to say too much. Only the following chapters can show whether or not the title is well chosen. I mention the matter here only to indicate that the character of the Gospel as the earliest major Christian martyrology has been one of the many surprises that have dawned on me as I have carried on this study.

Part One

THE CHARACTER OF THE CONVERSATION

O Hermes, preserve us from evil, for we
are all engaged in hermeneutics over
which you preside.[1]

In this book I invite you, as a reader, to engage with me in a fresh study of the Gospel called John. As a first step you should ask yourself what you expect to gain from such a study. Of possible expectations there is, of course, a wide range, but whatever it is that you expect will set the terms for the conversation between John and yourself. Do you expect from this Gospel a single, attractive portrait of Jesus? Or a complete account of his work among his people? Do you expect to cull out data from which to construct the core of Christian doctrines? Or the basic pattern of Christian duties? Do you plan to use John to provide stimuli for daily devotions or private prayer? Whatever your expectations may be, they will determine the range and depth of your dialogue with John. And should his concerns not coincide with your desires, even your best intentions are likely to die a speedy death.

Although I have used the terms conversation and dialogue, that may not be what happens when you open the Gospel. What happens is usually much less lively than a two-way conversation. When we open the Gospel we seldom view at the other end a human being—thinking, feeling, writing, hoping—but rather printed pages—impersonal, unresponsive, lifeless. Behind the

1

words we do not see a human face or sense the power of human emotions. And whoever is at the other end of this so-called conversation, we know full well that he did not have us in mind in what he was writing. So at our end, also, what happens falls far short of being an active participation in a dialogue. Because we are not directly addressed in what we read we become almost as anonymous, as faceless, as the author. Because he proves to be oblivious to our previous expectations, we return the courtesy by becoming equally oblivious to his concerns. Can we call the resulting interchange a conversation, when we compare it with the discussions at a dinner party or with our intense concentration in reading a personal letter? How can conversation flourish between two people who do not know each other and who are not interested in the same things? To use basketball jargon, fruitful reading requires that we go one-on-one with the author, but in this case the reader seldom meets the author. Result: frustration on both sides.

It has not always been so. John wrote his Gospel as part of a vigorous and dramatic two-way conversation. To his readers, he was no vague, anonymous, remote figure. In all probability, as we shall see, he was widely respected as an inspired leader. And to him, the first readers were well known as followers of Christ for whom he had been assigned major responsibility. Their concerns were of major concern to him. When he wrote to them he was trying to share with them messages from their common King, messages that could easily spell the difference between life and death. *Our* efforts at conversation with him may be inert and perfunctory. Not so *theirs.* It remains within the realm of possibility, then, for us to recover snatches of their ancient conversation. And it is altogether desirable for us to turn that possibility into actuality. Listening in on their dialogue may prove to be far less frustrating for us than going one-on-one with John. Because I am convinced of this I have divided this study into two parts. In Part One we will try to recover the skeletal structure of their conversation; that will enable us, in Part Two, to recover the substance of messages that John was charged to relay from the risen Lord to his followers in the churches.

Chapter I

THE NARRATOR

The prophetic experience is a sudden encounter
with the meaning behind events.[1]

Anything that is written has a writer. The writer chooses the
words, and in reading them we are responding to the writer. If
what is written is a narrative, we call the writer the narrator.
Even when the story deals with someone else, its primary purpose is to convey a message from the narrator to the audience
the narrator has chosen. To recapture the character of that conversation between the writer and the first readers of the Gospel
of John is our first major objective.

Nowhere does the narrator identify himself by name; calling him John is a later guess.* Nor does he intrude himself into
the story in an obvious way; the fact that readers seldom think of
him at all is a mark of his success in focusing attention on the
major characters. Yet, like all writers except official stenog-
raphers, John did leave his fingerprints, and in this chapter we
will locate some of them.[2]

The most obvious trace of his work is an occasional use of
the first person pronoun—in the opening chapter, for instance:
"And the Word . . . dwelt among *us*. . . ; *we* have beheld his glory,
glory as of the only Son from the Father [1:14]." Such a statement clearly implies that the entire opening confession should

---

*In referring to the author of the Gospel, I will use the masculine
pronouns he, his, him without prejudice as to sex. If readers prefer,
they may substitute feminine or neutral pronouns.

be read as "our" confession. The narrator is writing as a believer and as a member of a community of believers who have seen and bear witness to the glory of this Word, this Son. The choice of *we* rather than *I* suggests that the narrator is writing not only for himself but also as a representative of a larger group, either the whole company of believers or a limited group of its leaders who have been granted a vision of the glory. Decision on that point must await further analysis.

To identify the narrator as a believer is a more decisive step than many suppose. Belief implied a love for Jesus that entailed a commitment to his rigorous commands. To behold Jesus' glory entailed recognizing that his glorification had coincided with the hour of his crucifixion. The story of the crucifixion, as we shall see, defined believing as a readiness to share the same hostility and even the same death. The narrator could not have avoided applying that definition to himself. In fact his telling of the story is an action by which he expressed his own commitment to such obedience: "The Word . . . dwelt among *us*."

A second fingerprint may be found in a second use of the personal pronoun: "*We* speak of what *we* know, and give *our* testimony to what *we* have seen [3:11]." This statement is found in the discussion with Nicodemus, a teacher and ruler of Israel. In the discussion the words of Jesus turn almost without notice into the words of the narrator. "Truly, truly, I [Jesus] say to you [Nicodemus], we [the narrator] speak of what we know." The structure of the sentence is awkward because the present tense of Jesus becomes the present tense (we know) of the narrator, and that present tense becomes in turn an inclusive past (we have seen). In saying *we*, the narrator associates himself on the one hand with Jesus and on the other hand with other leaders who have seen and who now join in giving their testimonies. If he is not a member of the original band of witnesses, he views himself as one of their immediate successors. He also feels obliged to give testimony, if not to Nicodemus, then at least to those who, like Nicodemus, are teachers of Israel. It is also probable that his Christian readers would read his words as suggesting how they also might give their own testimonies to such teachers.

The paragraph that follows (3:16–21) can be read as a succinct summary of that joint testimony, because in many ways it fits more smoothly into the time frame of the narrator than into the earlier time frame of Jesus: "For God so loved the world that he gave (*aorist*/past tense) his only Son. . . . This is the judgment, that the light has come (perfect tense) into the world, . . . whoever does what is true comes (present tense) to the light." "Gave . . . has come"—in using these tenses John often indicates that he has in mind the whole story of Jesus, viewed in retrospect from his own time of writing. This becomes John's own testimony to his contemporaries—including the descendants of Nicodemus—and not only his own testimony but also that of other leaders for whom he serves as spokesman. We may safely infer that in writing the whole book, as also in writing this paragraph, the narrator was seeking to fulfill his own vocation as a witness. We may also consider it probable that his vocation was not limited to writing this book. Both before and after the composition of the Gospel, John was accustomed to giving oral testimonies in which he used the same significant *we*. This continuing vocation to and for his readers is clearly indicated in two later texts as well (19:35 and 20:31; cf. below, pp. 71, 80). The Gospel should, in fact, be read as a document that began its life as a series of testimonies that had first been given orally.

It is possible that another passage reflects the narrator's perspective on what he is doing. This passage occurs at a dramatic moment near the end of the Gospel, when the high priest was subjecting Jesus to a final interrogation. The prosecutor shows as much interest in the disciples as in Jesus: "The high priest then questioned Jesus *about his disciples* and his teaching [18:19]." That implies that the disciples were on trial in the trial of Jesus. So how did Jesus reply? He first spoke of his teaching, how he had spoken in full publicity in synagogues and in the temple (cf. below, pp. 32–33). Then he spoke of his disciples and of their obligation to answer for themselves: "Why do you ask me? Ask those who have heard me, what I have said to them; they know what I said [18:21]." Here Jesus may have been referring to the Pharisees who had heard him teaching. That is how many interpreters construe this answer. However, we should remember that in the preceding five chapters the disciples had been his only auditors. They alone knew what he had said, and after his death they would be responsible for answering such interrogations. I think that here the narrator is skillfully deflecting attention away from Jesus to his disciples, and from this trial to later trials under Caiaphas and his successors. Unless we bring the disciples into the story as those who "know what I said" (cp. 3:11 and 14:26), the query of the high priest is left hanging in the air. That is not the narrator's usual way of telling a story.

I draw two inferences from such a reading of Jesus' answer. First, the next verses show that at the original trial the disciples, as represented by Peter, had been too panic-stricken to reply. John is brutal in showing this failure on their part to give their answer to Jesus' answer. Second, the story points beyond the Passion to the time when disciples would belatedly accept their responsibility to tell what Jesus had said. It also points ahead to the time when the narrator, by telling the whole story, would provide the answer in written form. "They know what I have said to them; ask them." The Gospel may be read as a way by which the narrator gave that answer, his account of all that Jesus had said that had inevitably led to trial and death. It is John's *martyria,* a story of Jesus' condemnation by the Jews in which his own condemnation was implicated.

The work of the narrator is further illuminated by Jesus' farewell promises to his disciples: "These things I have spoken to you, while I am still with you. But the Counselor, the Holy Spirit, whom the Father will send in my name, he will teach you all things, and will bring to your remembrance all that I have said to you [14:25–26]." Here the time frame is definitely the period after Jesus' death, and that surely includes the time in which John is telling his story. Although Jesus gave this promise to such men as Peter and the beloved disciple, those are the very men whom the narrator claims to represent (21:24). According to this text, the Spirit will enable them to recall "all that I have said to you," words that describe the contents of the Gospel itself. To Christians, the reference to the Counselor was not to something foreign or bizarre, nor to formal dogma, but to an intimate gift: "You know him, for he dwells with you, and will be in you [14:17]." When the narrator claimed to be relaying tradition received from the beloved disciple, it would be strange indeed if he did not trace that tradition to this promise: "When the

Counselor comes, . . . even the Spirit of truth, . . . he will bear witness to me; and you also are witnesses, because you have been with me from the beginning [15:26–27]." Writing his Gospel is one way by which the narrator relies on the witness given by "the Spirit of truth." Thus there is abundant evidence for the conclusion of M. de Jonge:

> The Gospel is an essential component of the Spirit's testimony. . . . [It is] the result of the teaching and recalling activity of the Spirit within the community of disciples leading to a deeper and fuller insight into all that Jesus as the Son revealed during his stay on earth.[3]

These texts force us to recognize that the narrator thought of himself as a recipient of this Spirit. It is true, of course, that within this community all believers had been baptized with the same Spirit (3:6); yet the community also recognized the importance of such specialized gifts as that of prophecy. "In the Judaism of the time," writes Joachim Jeremias, "the imparting of the Spirit almost always means prophetic inspiration: a man is grasped by God, who authorizes him to be his messenger and preaches and speaks through him."[4] We can safely conclude, then, that the narrator probably viewed himself as a prophet and that he was recognized as such among his churches. Because he nowhere says this about himself, it must remain a hypothesis, though one that is defended by an increasing number of scholars.[5] But to call him a prophet means little unless we are clear about the basic task of an early Christian prophet. Eugene Boring has summarized that task thus: "The early Christian prophet was an immediately inspired spokesman for the risen Jesus who received intelligible oracles that he felt impelled to deliver to the Christian community."[6] Such a summary may not seem to fit precisely the work of John in writing the Gospel, for its chapters do not have the form of spoken oracles; yet they reflect many of the functions of the prophet, such as the following:

- a prophet is made intensely aware of the powerful presence of the risen Lord;
- is charged to tell God's people what has been seen and heard from that Lord;

- serves the people as a leader in their worship;
- instructs them in the commands and the way of the Lord;
- relays to the community the traditions received from Jesus, both before and after his death;
- screens the memories of the Messiah through various passsages of scripture and vice versa;
- helps Christians understand their own situations in the light of their participation in the stories of Jesus' death and glorification.

The Gospel does these things and many more, and each of them is a mark of prophetic vocation. In the following chapters we will notice other marks which lead us to join Boring in his judgment:

> The author of the Gospel himself functions as such a prophet, uniting the tradition from Jesus with the present address of the risen Jesus in an inseparable bond. . . . The tradition is made present by the charisma; the charisma is made valid by the tradition.[7]

As a prophet, the narrator was an important link in the chain of communication that reached from God through the crucified and risen Christ, through the Spirit of truth, through the first disciples, to communities of believers engaged in worship. The Jesus who had come from God is the Son who had gone to the Father.* The martyr who had won his victory over the world was the Lord who had given his Spirit to his disciples; the Spirit that had been given to those first disciples had continued to furnish the church with all charismatic gifts. That chain of communication was nothing less than the lifeline of the early churches, in which the continuing work of prophets was essential. In no later century of church history would the role of prophets be so strategic. This is made clear by Gerd Theissen's analysis: "The internal structure of the Jesus movement was determined by the

---

*Readers may have noticed my use of the two related metaphors, Son and Father, to refer to Jesus and God. Those metaphors have recently been singled out as being sexist and exclusive. Such a deficiency would not, of course, have occurred to the participants in the original dialogue. Because I am concerned with that original dialogue I have continued the metaphors. The metaphorical structure is integral to the thought of the Gospel.

interaction of three roles: the wandering charismatics, their sympathizers in the local communities, and the bearer of revelation [the risen Lord]."[8] The Gospel must be viewed as the narrator's Spirit-guided conversation with his churches, through which he was convinced that the risen Lord was speaking to those same churches. This becomes clearest of all perhaps in the Farewell Address in chapters 13–17. As David E. Aune writes: "The discourses of the Johannine Jesus bear unmistakable marks of having been formulated by prophetic or charismatic individuals within the context of the pneumatic worship of the Johannine community."[9] No less than Jesus did this narrator have a high regard for those shepherds "to whom the word of God came [10:35]."[10]

Few recent studies of the Gospel have been as thorough and perceptive as that of B. Olsson, who places under the microscope the Evangelist's way of dealing with the tradition. According to Olsson, the Evangelist filtered all sayings and events through a double screen—through the story of Jesus' death and through the scripture as used in the churches. In both respects he was aided in this work of interpretation by the Paraclete, who "is the great exegete and interpreter of Jesus' words and actions."[11]

The role of the narrator was not simply that of a prophetic spokesman of the risen Lord; it was also that of a literary editor, fitting together bits and pieces of tradition into a more-or-less coherent account. Any storyteller finds it difficult to avoid making comments on the story while telling it, comments that may be separated from the account of what happened. In John these parenthetical comments are numerous and often extensive. They may be found in every chapter except in the unbroken dialogue of chapters 14 and 15 and in the prayer of chapter 17. From these asides much can be inferred about both the narrator and his readers.[12] I cannot review the whole body of these comments, but I will cite a few samples.

In some cases the narrator simply keeps the reader in touch with Jesus' movements from one place to another (e.g., "Bethany was near Jerusalem [11:18]") or from one time to another (e.g., "when he was in Jerusalem [2:23]"). Care is taken to peg many incidents at particular festivals (e.g., "The Passover of the Jews was at hand [2:13]"). The narrator identifies the major characters and links together different scenes in which they appear (e.g., "It was Mary who anointed the Lord [11:2]"). He explains data that might be unfamiliar or unclear (e.g., "His disciples had gone away into the city to buy food [4:8]"). Comments of this sort are routine tasks for any narrator. But this editor often makes much more significant remarks. For example, he points out how events are related to scriptural prophecies, so that prediction and fulfillment interpret each other (e.g., "His disciples remembered that it was written, 'Zeal for your house will consume me [2:17]'"). Similarly, he calls attention to the fulfillment of Jesus' own prediction (2:22) and even to an unwitting prediction made by Caiaphas (11:51). Thus the editor helps readers recall a long sequence in the fulfillments of prophecies: the scripture, John the Baptist, Nathanael, Jesus, Caiaphas. And he mentions prophecies whose fulfillment still lies ahead, in the coming presence and work of the Holy Spirit (16:13).

Not only does the editor call attention to the fulfillment of verbal predictions; there are also many actions whose meaning is not revealed until long after they happen. Some of these actions are called signs (4:52); some stress Jesus' knowledge of the hearts of believers both before (6:64) and after (20:9) his arrest; others center in the self-deceptions and cowardice of disciples (6:71). Jesus knew what the future would hold, and the narrator shares this knowledge with him (7:39). Other editorial asides point to the motives of adversaries (e.g., "This was why the Jews persecuted Jesus, because he did this on the sabbath [5:16]"). The editor explains why premature efforts of Jesus' opponents failed (7:30) and indicates when the final conspiracy was hatched (11:53). So the editor provides the thread by which episodes are stitched together.

As spokesman for the community of believers he formulates their common faith: "You worship what you do not know; we worship what we know [4:22]." Some of these testimonies are given to such adversaries as "a ruler of the Jews" (3:14, 16–21, 31–36); others represent liturgical or creedal forms that were used within services of worship. A prime example of these is the Prologue, which is not only a summary of the entire Gospel, not only a poetic affirmation of the origin of the prophetic Word, but also a simple communal doxology: "From his fulness we have all received [1:16]."

Such comments often, although not invariably, reflect the time and place where the Gospel was being written. They serve to introduce the reader into the middle of the events being recounted and, simultaneously, to introduce those events into the imagination of a worshiping audience. The expertness of the narrator may be judged by the fact that few readers become conscious of the perspective within which the story is told. Few are aware of the degree to which the narrator is the one speaking in the Prologue, the one who introduces the actors, who explains their inner thoughts, who provides the settings for the dialogues, who sees the end from the beginning, and who interprets the beginning on the basis of his knowledge of the end.

The more one detects such traces of the editor's work, the more one comes to realize that "the narrator's distinctive point of view controls the reader's perception of Jesus" so that a reader soon accepts him "as a reliable guide to the meaning of Jesus' life and death."[13] The story presupposes the omniscience of the narrator and the reader's acceptance of that omniscience. For instance, the narrator presumes to know verbatim the words of Jesus' prayer to his Father, to remember them infallibly and to relay them to his readers many years later. This omniscience is anchored in part to the retrospective stance of an editor who looks back on events from a later time and can interpret those events in ways not possible earlier. We have been taught to be suspicious of distortions that arise from such a retrospect, and we need, perhaps, the caution voiced by George B. Caird: "Important events do not disclose their full significance to the participants at the time of the occurrence. A couple celebrating their Golden Wedding . . . have a knowledge of 'what actually happened' which was inaccessible to them as bride and groom."[14]

We should also recall that John was more than an editor charged with recounting earlier events; he was a prophet called to trace those events to their hidden origins in the will of God and to provide spiritual guidance for God's people. The prophet's story must encourage both distance and involvement on the part of readers. Because the events disclose the will of

God the readers are given a stance outside the course of events; yet they are encouraged to identify themselves with the participants in those events, with Philip or Mary or Nicodemus. A sense of distance is conveyed by looking at specific episodes within the horizons of Jesus' coming from and his going to the Father. At the same time, a sense of involvement is conveyed to the degree that readers view their own work within similar brackets: "As the Father sent me, even so I send you [20:21]." "The Hebrew genius for the narrative," writes U. Simon, "has an uncanny bent towards welding nearness to the action with distance to the spectator. . . . The narrator is near the fire . . . he mediates it in such a way that we look at it from outside and from far off."[15] In short, as editor, John is telling in sequence a series of past events, and as prophet, he is revealing the significance of those events. In technical terms, he is fulfilling the demand for hermeneutics. He interprets past events in such a way as to span the temporal distance between *then* and *now,* and he interprets the events of salvation in such a way as to span the a-temporal distance between the glorified Lord and the worshiping church. Because he is doing both of these things simultaneously, each historical narrative becomes "a symbolic narrative . . . with many allusive elements."[16]

Any examination of the editorial asides found in the Gospel raises the question of whether we can distinguish between the position adopted by the narrator and "what actually happened." Once the question is raised, the answer becomes inescapable: There is such a complete correlation between the words of the narrator and the words of his major character that they cannot be separated. "Jesus and the narrator share the same vocabulary and use the same terms with a veiled or double meaning."[17] We must therefore recognize the fact that in the composition of the Gospel there is a complex fusion of at least four sources: the Jesus who had been baptized with the Spirit, the Paraclete who had been given by Jesus to his disciples after his glorification, those disciples as represented by the beloved disciple, and the narrator who relayed that shared tradition to his audience. The Gospel is written under the assumption that these four sources form a chain of command that links the living God to the readers. Usually when the narrator speaks of the word (*logos;* cf. below, chapter IX) he has in mind that entire chain.

The discourses in John cannot and do not intend to be historical reporting of a word-for-word record. [They are] the words of the risen Lord from on high, addressing his community on earth through an inspired Evangelist, conscious of his charismatic enlightenment from the Holy Spirit.[18]

Chapter II

THE FIRST READERS

Israel has no ethnic meaning unless the
presence of God remains with the people.[1]

Because the narrator directed his statements to a particular
audience, it will be impossible for us to understand his half of
that conversation unless we understand their half. The more
actively we listen to his story as they listened to it, the greater will
be the degree of our understanding. As J. Louis Martyn insists,
if we are to understand John, "we must make every effort to take
up temporary residence in the Johannine community."[2] As the
Buddhist koan reminds us, "Two hands make this noise
[clapping]; how much noise does one hand make?"

So the problem becomes how best to go about recovering
their half of the conversation when none of their words is cited
directly. We can safely assume that there was enough rapport
between speaker and listeners to make communication possible
and enough divergence to make it desirable. We should ask,
then, about the character of this rapport.

First, we can be confident that the partners in this conversation were bound together by their belief in Jesus and their commitment to follow him. Like the narrator, the listeners were
Christians, accustomed to worship together, to sing and pray
together, to listen to the scripture and to the messages from their
charismatic leaders. To take up residence in this community is to

reckon with its lively sense of God's presence and in fact to grant a high priority to that presence. As Morris L. West writes: "Once you accept the existence of God—however you define him, however you explain your relationship to him—then you are caught forever with His presence at the center of all things."[3] And for John this centering down was more than a matter of presence; it was a matter of parenthood. They had all been born "not of blood, nor of the will of the flesh, nor of human will, but of God [1:13]." A sign of this birth was baptism in the Spirit, which separated them from all others as it united them in a single family (1:33; 3:5–8). Their common life had received a new center and had been set within new horizons. Together they submitted to daily guidance by the Spirit. Such guidance linked them directly to the redemptive acts of God that had been done in the past and equally to those that were to be done in the future. Nothing characterized their common life better than their "worship in spirit and truth" (4:22–24). As the setting of that confession indicates, to worship in spirit destroyed the previously strong attachment to such sacred places as Jerusalem and Gerizim by establishing a stronger attachment to their new habitat, the realm of the Holy Spirit. "The presence of the Spirit within the community was the central phenomenon which convinced Christians that the eschaton [the event of deliverance and liberation] had in some way arrived in the person of Jesus of Nazareth."[4]

The dynamics of congregational worship were such as to release many charismatic gifts, among which the gift of prophecy was prominent. And wherever the gift of prophecy appeared there appeared also the gift of discerning what the Spirit was saying through the prophets. These were twin gifts—prophecy and discernment—that together enabled a congregation to hear the word of the risen Jesus and see his works.[5] So in writing his Gospel, John could count on readers who had been born again through the Spirit, who had been baptized in the Spirit, who had been engaged in worshiping in the Spirit, and who had thereby received the gift of discernment.

In all probability his audience was composed in large part of *Jewish* believers in the Messiah. They had felt at home in the sabbath worship in the synagogues. Their memories were stocked with the funded experience of Israel from its beginnings. Their language was saturated with the prayers of the psalms, with the litanies of humble devotion. Their minds were structured by the sabbath readings from the Law and the Prophets. Their calendars gave priority to the festivals and feasts of the temple. Their imaginations reverberated with the legends of patriarchs and kings. They brought this rich heritage with them when they received the Spirit. Perhaps they thought of themselves symbolically as sitting under the fig tree, like Nathanael when Jesus had first seen him. In response they had hailed him as "King of Israel" (1:49f.). Or like the blind man whom he had healed, their testimony to his power had provoked collisions with parents and scribes (9:1ff.). Each believer had first heard about Jesus from a fellow Jew and had become a potential witness to other Jews. Each had become a member of a Christian cell, perhaps within, perhaps separate from, the earlier synagogue. This cell, as well as its individual members, was charged with testifying that Jesus was in fact a prophet like Moses whom God had promised to send to Israel (Deuteronomy 18:15).[6]

We have said that John was bound to these readers by their common possession of the Spirit, their gift of discernment that enabled them to comprehend his gift of prophecy. Now we may add that this bond of the Spirit was inseparable from the bond of the Word. Jesus himself had identified the Spirit with his words (6:63). So too the narrator in his opening confession: "the Word . . . dwelt among us . . . we beheld his glory . . . from his fulness we have all received [1:14, 16]." Just as believers had received life through the Spirit, they had received life through this indwelling Word, which linked Jesus to John and John to all his readers. The common bond meant that the conversation could proceed at a deep level, not from mouth to ear but from heart to heart, or better, from Spirit to Spirit. This, in fact, may have been the reason the narrator began the Gospel with such a prologue. Its major function is neither apologetic nor polemic, but confessional and doxological. In tracing the movement of the Word from its beginning with God to its presence with "us," the Prologue constituted an act of praise that bound the absent narrator to his present listeners. In familiar, homespun words it pointed to the mysteries that inhered in their family life as children who had been born of the same parent (cf. below, p. 100).

John's listeners appear quite clearly in the climactic paragraph of Jesus' prayer in chapter 17.[7] The sequence of three paragraphs is significant. In the first paragraph (vv. 1–5) Jesus prays for the completion of his own work in the hour when the glorification of the Father will coincide with the glorification of the Son. In the second paragraph (vv. 6–19) Jesus intercedes for those disciples among whom he is standing. They will be glorified in the completion of their mission as given by him. Already they have received his logos; he is now consecrating them for work in the world after his death, as mediators of the same logos.[8]

In the third paragraph (vv. 20–26) Jesus shifts his attention to another group—"those who believe in me through their logos." Here he distinguishes between the disciples as mediators of the logos and believers as its recipients. Believers will not have seen Jesus but will be bound to him by three power-laden gifts: the logos (vv. 6, 14, 17), the name (vv. 6, 11, 12), and the glory (vv. 4, 10). In so phrasing the prayer I think the narrator has in mind believers in his own day who will take special joy and courage from being included within the circle of Jesus' intercession. To be sure, most interpreters think of this paragraph as having a much more general reference. Rudolf Bultmann, for example, understands the second paragraph as referring not alone "to the preaching of the first generation, but to Christian preaching in general," and he understands the third paragraph as referring to "all believers without reference to space and time."[9] It is natural for modern readers to assume this, because we are so far removed from the initial conversation, and every successive generation of believers has included itself within the range of Jesus' concern. Yet this way of construing the text does violence to the original situation when John wanted to help specific believers to meet specific dilemmas. To generalize his audience is to lose sight of those dilemmas.

Those believers were in fact facing an unprecedented range of challenges, for the messengers whom Jesus had first commissioned had disappeared from the scene, leaving the rest without their leaders. We can only speculate concerning the nature of

17

some of those challenges, but such speculation can hardly be avoided. Because many of Jesus' messengers had been murdered as Peter had been, it is almost certain that their followers were more exposed than ever to similar dangers. And now that they could no longer rely on those who had been with Jesus, their own memories of him would almost certainly become vaguer and less dependable. The lack of authoritative agents for Jesus would almost certainly mean that dissensions within the church would become more explosive and less tractable. Charismatic leaders, undisciplined by reliable memories, would now pull in different directions and believers would become confused. How could they test the authority of new leaders? How could they overcome the tensions with unbelieving families and neighbors? In the face of continuing persecution should they take the safer or the more dangerous line?

> But say, if our Deliverer up to Heaven
> Must reascend, what will betide the few,
> His faithful, left among the unfaithful herd,
> The enemies of truth; who then shall guide
> His people, who defend? Will they not deal
> Worse with his followers than with him they dealt?
> "Be sure they will," said the Angel.[10]

Probably the narrator, like his readers, knew firsthand the painful vacuum that was left by the death of Peter and the beloved disciple (chapter 21). Like his readers, John would have been reassured by Jesus' prayer and by his promise to dwell with them no less than with Thomas or Philip. Because he would have been aware of a quite specific cluster of needs, John would have addressed those needs in editing the words of Jesus and in telling the story of his work among "the Jews." He knew firsthand the struggles of believers against unbelief, the evanescence of their first excitements through the passing of time, the confusions as well as the confidences released by the charismatic gifts, the continuing eruption of fears provoked by the hostility of former friends. John was keenly aware of such challenges, and this awareness colored the stories he told.

The book functions for its readers in precisely the same way that the epiphany of its hero functions within its narratives and dialogues. . . . It is a book for insiders, for if one already

18

belonged to the Johannine community, then we may presume that its manifold bits of tradition would be familiar.[11]

Because this was a book for insiders, in reading it they would know more than the actors themselves had known. They would know, for example, who the betrayer was, even before Peter did, and they would know why Peter and Thomas had misunderstood what Jesus meant by "the way." In this sense, readers could feel superior even to the disciples, whom they revered as heroes. Yet, in another sense, the story would help the readers recognize their own inability to go where Jesus was going. They would appreciate Jesus' unreadiness to trust those who believed too easily or quickly (2:23–24). They would find their own fears mirrored in the believers who kept their faith hidden from the Jews. The Gospel would make them aware of many kinds of self-deception and confusion of which believers were capable, would help them realize that believing is a matter of many degrees and many stages. So John was writing to believers in order that they might come to believe in such a way that they would have "life in his name [20:31]."

We must now return to a point already noted, to the distinction in Jesus' prayer between intercession for the disciples and intercession for believers. There is ample evidence to show that this distinction was a significant element in Johannine thought. Yet few modern readers take note of this distinction, because it has become our habit to suppose that the two terms are synonymous and interchangeable—all disciples are believers and vice versa. Ever since Luke wrote his two volumes this literary convention has become virtually universal.[12] But that was not true of either Mark[13] or Matthew.[14] And it was not true of John. In his story several important differences exist between the two groups.

For one thing, the disciples were itinerants who joined Jesus in walking from Judea to Samaria to Galilee and back again. As this group traveled from town to town they kept the funds and were expected to provide food both for Jesus (4:8, 31, 13:29) and for the crowds (6:5–9; 21:10, 15). Such a footloose existence was not demanded of all believers. Moreover, Jesus clearly trained these disciples to carry out special assignments. He put his flock in their care; if they should fail to risk their lives for the sheep, they would become day laborers and not shepherds (10:12–13; 21:15–17). Disciples were related to believers as shepherds were to sheep. Other metaphors expressed similar distinctions:

> disciples: believers :: harvesters: grain
> disciples: believers :: fishermen: fish
> disciples: believers :: branches: grapes

The two groups were quite separate, with one group depending on the other.

These special tasks required special resources. The disciples became Jesus' *own* in a special sense (13:1), because they were to be sent by him as he had been sent by the Father (13:16). He delegated his authority to them. They baptized in his name (4:1–2). They gathered up the fragments of bread and fish after the supper in the wilderness (6:12). They forgave or retained sins. He promised them that they would do even greater works and that they would receive whatever help they might need. The gift of the Paraclete would enable them to cope with all emergencies. The narrator tells the stories of Judas and Peter as if the betrayal of a disciple's trust was much more horrible than any wavering on the part of a believer.

In giving disciples these gifts, their master made them vulnerable to special dangers. They would inherit the enmity that had greeted Jesus. To be his disciple required that one risk one's life both for the sake of Jesus and for the sake of those very enemies (13:12–17, 35–38; 15:12–20). Only in fulfilling this assignment would they receive his gifts of peace, joy, glory, and power (cf. below, chapter VI). The whole period of their specialized training reached its climax when Jesus manifested himself to them after his death, breathed on them the Holy Spirit, and sent them into the harvest field.

When we recall John's story as a whole we find many more believers than disciples and more disciples than the twelve, a group that appears on the stage only rarely and incidentally (6:67–71; 20:24). For this picture of the disciples as a distinct group of trainees, the Gospel provides two analogues. One analogue is the group of disciples gathered by John the Baptist, in which case the narrator visualized a master prophet surrounded by a school of fledgling prophets (3:25—4:1). The other analogue is that of the Pharisees who spoke of themselves as disciples of Moses (9:28). In John's day Moses was viewed as a master prophet, teacher, and lawgiver, in loyalty to whom disciples carried out specific tasks in the synagogues, teaching and interpreting his revelation. These two analogues support the conclusion that, in Jesus' case as well, the band of disciples should be viewed as prophets, teachers, and interpreters of scripture, whose specialized vocations separated them from the larger group of believers.

This distinction was important to both the narrator and his listeners. We read of many occasions when people are said to believe but they do not then become disciples (2:23; 3:12–16; 4:46–54; 9:38; 10:38, 42; 11:25, 40, 45f.; 12:36–44). There are still other instances in which the disciples are said not to believe (2:21–22; 6:60; 11:15). In fact, John seems to make a special point of noticing the varying degrees of belief among the disciples, as symbolized by portraits of Judas, Peter, Thomas, Philip, Nathanael and the beloved disciple.

However, the narrator does not in every instance maintain this distinction between believers and disciples. Joseph of Arimathea, for example, is called a disciple, although there is no evidence that he belonged to the group of itinerant leaders, at least not before Jesus' death (19:38). The brothers of Jesus appear not to have made the distinction between the two categories (7:3–5). These exceptions to the rule may indicate that the narrator did not always recast the stories he used to make them reflect his own thinking. Or the exceptions may show that the line between the two categories was not rigid but could be crossed from time to time.

Yet John's basic attitude toward the disciples is clear. As prophets and teachers, they were being trained by Jesus for special assignments and charged to continue his revelation of God's activity. As witnesses who had been with Jesus "from the beginning," they had left homes and occupations to travel full time with him. As delegates, they carried his authority to proclaim God's word and to accomplish God's works. The power of the Holy Spirit enabled them to cope with this assignment even as it brought down the world's hatred on them.

I have stressed this concept of the disciples partly because it helps us to distinguish the narrator from many of his readers. Of the two groups, he identified himself more closely with disciples than with believers. Burnett H. Streeter was right to observe that John "was regarded, by himself, and by the church for which he wrote, as an inspired prophet."[15] This fact becomes clear in the personal pronouns that he used in the closing verses: "This is the disciple . . . who has written these things; and *we* know that his testimony is true [21:24]." In using the term *we,* the narrator distinguished himself both from the beloved disciple and from his readers. Yet he links his words closely to that disciple's testimony. Those who listened to his words became dependent on the narrator for linking their faith to the testimony of the original band of disciples. As believers, they received the logos through an unbroken chain of command.

A more important point may be gained by recognizing the unique role of the disciples: It helps us to identify a significant bloc of John's readers.[16] In constructing his Gospel the narrator had a special message for the charismatic leaders in his churches. In giving them the Holy Spirit, the risen Lord had made them the immediate successors to the original cast of disciples. It is well to recall here an earlier observation concerning the tripartite shape of early Palestinian churches: the divine revealer, the charismatic guides, the rank-and-file believers (cf. above, pp. 8–9). John did not forget the needs of those believers, for the sheep in this flock were a prime concern of the master shepherd. Yet the fate of the flock depended on the faithfulness of their shepherds, who were, like the narrator himself, successors to the first group of fishermen, harvesters, prophets, teachers. So the narrator presents the farewell conversations[17] with Jesus in such a way that these charismatic leaders would recognize their own tasks, temptations, and resources. In Jesus' prayer for his first disciples (17:6–19) they would detect his continuing intercession for them, so long as they continued to reveal his logos, whether to believers or to unbelievers.

To sum up, then, we visualize two distinct constituencies in the original readership of the Gospel: the narrator's fellow-believers and his charismatic colleagues. Before we complete the study I will supply ample evidence that he was thoroughly acquainted with the difficulties and the opportunities of both groups. His insights stemmed in part from the fact that he had firsthand knowledge of the adversaries of those two groups. So, to share that knowledge, we must examine the position of those adversaries.

Chapter III

THE ADVERSARIES

The greatest enemies of religion have
always been religious people themselves.[1]

Throughout the Gospel, readers are confronted with one and
only one adversarial group. To be sure, there may be differences
among adversaries but not at the point of hostility to Jesus and
his disciples. We locate this group by the telltale use of pronouns.
As we have found help in the pronouns we and you, in recaptur-
ing the conversation between narrator and readers, so similar
help is provided by the use of third-person pronouns: they,
them, their. At no point is this help closer to the surface than in
four statements in chapter 16 (vv. 1–3), each of which carries
numerous implications.[2]

> 1. "I have said all this to you to keep you from falling away.
> 2. They will put you out of the synagogues;
> 3. indeed, the hour is coming when whoever kills you will
>   think he is offering service to God.
> 4. And they will do this because they have not known the
>   Father, nor me."

I will comment on each of these statements.

1. Here Jesus speaks in the first person to his disciples, although, as we have seen, the narrator had in mind the prophetic
successors of those disciples. The locale is the upper room. The
time is the end of their instruction period in preparation for the
dangerous period after the Master's death. The words *all this*

24

surely refer to everything that he has said in this particular speech, beginning in 15:1 and ending in 16:33. In all likelihood the narrator also had in mind the entire Farewell Address and perhaps the entire legacy of Jesus' teaching. The intercessory prayer for these same disciples obviously focused on the same ominous prospect (17:14). The text assumes that after Jesus' own martyrdom they would face a similar test because of their loyalty to him. A careless reader might suppose that the chief danger was a violent death; to Jesus, however, the far greater danger was that of stumbling over the rock of offense. The disciples' fear of death might become so strong as to induce them to betray him. Throughout the New Testament "the stone on which men stumble" was thought of as the death of Jesus. Not to fall away, not to stumble, meant that his disciples, because of their memory of him, would accept their own deaths as a form of testifying to his victory over death. Conversely, to fall away in craven dread of death meant that his mission had failed, because they would have forfeited their own mission. So interpreted, this first I-you sentence prepares the way for the second you-they sentence.

2. Here the adversaries are clearly identified as the authorities in the synagogues who wield power to exclude persons from worship there. It is also clear that this exclusion is no act of arbitrary individual pique. The rulers have enough support from other members of the synagogues to ban these disciples. Their authority is buttressed by tradition, prestige, status, and scriptural legitimacy. The prediction anticipates situations after Jesus' own death and identifies the future adversaries of disciples with former adversaries of Jesus. "If they persecuted me, they will persecute you [15:20]." Accordingly, this statement encourages readers to listen to the story of Jesus' Passion as a vignette of their own suffering.

The second statement (they . . . you) also implies that the disciples (and their successors in John's day) had once been regular worshipers in the synagogue. It had formed their native habitat, their spiritual home; to be driven out would have been traumatic. Only if that were so would exclusion have been an effective sanction that would cause some to fall away. For them, exclusion from their spiritual home would be a form of dying. Probably these disciples would have agreed with Paul: "They are Israelites, and to them belong the sonship, the glory, the covenants, the giving of the law, the worship, and the promises [Rom. 9:4]." Hostility from these "Israelites" created a genuine crisis: Disciples were forced to choose between life within the synagogue and life in Christ.

3. The third statement brings into play an even more drastic sanction: the threat of death at the hands of these authorities. Here each phrase has potent implications, and none more potent than the first: "The hour is coming." Anyone who is familiar with this Gospel immediately recognizes the importance of this *hour* (along with the cognate terms *the day* and *the time*). The hour is the time set by God for the fulfillment of God's purpose and calling. As applied to Jesus, this hour signaled the fulfillment of his mission by means of death and glorification. On various early occasions John had observed that Jesus' time had not yet come, but he introduced the Passover discourse with the announcement, "Jesus knew that his hour had come [13:1]." So when Jesus used the same words to announce the death of his disciples, he effectively established a direct linkage between his death and theirs, his vocation in death and their vocation. To be sure, their deaths would come years later, yet they would nevertheless share the same *hour.*

This linkage derives from God's purpose, an accent that may be indicated by the simple conjunction when ("the hour is coming *when*"). The English conjunction when suggests only a future time, but the Greek conjunction *hina* has a more complex set of nuances. It usually is used to introduce a purpose or a result clause. In three other places in John, *hina* is used with *the hour* (12:23; 13:1; 16:32). All these texts contain an element of purpose that should be preserved. God has a purpose in setting the hour for both Jesus and his disciples; the violence of their enemies will be instrumental in the fulfillment of that purpose. The *when* is also an *in order that.*

"When whoever kills you . . ."—this is not an independent but a subordinate clause; the more important clause follows. This means that the narrator's accent falls not on the act of murder but on the justification given for that act. Even so, the act of murder sets a high boundary between the two groups: *They* are murderers; *you*, their victims. This is obviously an empirical social boundary, separating a powerful majority from a powerless minority, those inside from those outside a dominant religious community. The empirical boundary marks an even more decisive psychic boundary, a radical inner and outer alienation that is expressed—at least on one side—in irrepressible religious hatred. It is also a moral boundary that separates those who are willing to kill from those who are willing to be killed. Death had the same meaning for both groups—and yet a very different significance.

"Whoever kills you will think he is offering service to God." Here the narrator marks out what he considers the most decisive boundary of all. Both murderers and murdered will be motivated by the desire to serve God. Which party is in the right? If *they* are right, *we* must *fall away*. To *them*, Judas is a hero who recognized the truth in the nick of time. The story of Peter during the trial of Jesus illustrates the power of the pressures exerted by this religious group. So too does Paul's admission of his own opposition to Jesus' disciples: He too had been "as to the law a Pharisee, as to zeal a persecutor of the church, as to righteousness under the law blameless [Phil. 3:5–6]."

We can conjure up few trials that would have been more conducive to "falling away." To risk death at the hands of strangers is one thing, but death at the hands of friends, neighbors, and devout companions from one's ancestral home is quite another. To accept death from pagans is one thing but from venerated disciples of Moses, to whom God has entrusted the guidance of the people, is quite another. Now the refusal to fall away requires at least a plausible explanation of why God's servants are ready to kill you and why you should be ready to accept death at their hands. For that explanation John turns to the fourth statement, which is perhaps the most climactic of all (yet one that interpreters often overlook).

Before turning to the fourth statement we should pause to examine recent discussions of the Gospel that have this in common: a neglect of the third and fourth statements. We find in these first three statements a mounting climax; that is, the prospect of death is a more extreme penalty than the prospect of exclusion from the synagogue. Yet Raymond Brown is typical of many recent interpreters who find greater significance in the threat of exclusion from the synagogue. That threat reflects "the Church-Synagogue polemic at the end of the century." Accordingly, Brown treats the reference to martyrdom in the third statement "as almost parenthetical, interrupting the flow of thought from 2 to 4."[3] So too Barnabas Lindars writes: "Jesus gives some slight [sic] idea of the nature of the persecution to be expected."[4] It is hard to understand why these scholars should turn away from the obvious Johannine accent on the third statement, especially when we recall such episodes as the stoning of Stephen (Acts 7:54—8:3) and the stoning of Paul (2 Corinthians 11:25), both at the hands of the religious authorities and both treated as typical rather than as unusual incidents. To minimize the brutal truth of the third statement is to minimize the hatreds exemplified in the death of Jesus as well as the pressures on his disciples to fall away. It also diminishes the narrator's own accent on the fourth statement, to which we now turn.

4. "They will do this because they have not known the Father, nor me." Why should this explanation be so essential to the prophecy? The tenses are significant. The future tense, *will do this,* looks forward to martyrdoms taking place after Jesus' death. The aorist tense, *have not known,* looks backward from that future action to that hour when knowledge of both the Father and his Son had become accessible. That is to say, the future enemies of the disciples would look back on Jesus' crucifixion without recognizing that God had actually been revealed in that event as Jesus' Father. They would kill his disciples because, to them, the criminal execution of Jesus had excluded such a possibility. Only this judgment concerning the death of Jesus could explain their mistaken conviction that the service of God required the murder of Jesus' messengers.

At issue was the simultaneous identity of God as Jesus' Father and of Jesus as Son of that Father. The statement places in sharpest contrast *their* God and *my* Father. Which God is the Father? Who is his Son? (Later, on pp. 108–10, we will examine further Johannine distinctions between the two words, God and

Father.) The Johannine narrative makes these two questions inseparable. In fact, no verse in scripture so clearly points to the radical changes in the content of the word *God* that were made necessary by the death of Jesus. Jurgen Moltmann writes: "Faith in the 'crucified God' is also a contradiction of everything men have ever conceived, desired and sought to be assured of by the term 'God.'"[5] Disciples accepted that contradiction; their adversaries rejected it. Martyrdom measured the incompatibility of acceptance and rejection. This is surely why the narrator introduced the prophecy with the loaded words "the hour is coming," because the message conveyed by the disciples' martyrdom would coincide with the message conveyed by his. For the disciples to fall away would signal their acceptance of the God of their enemies and their denial of this Son as revealer of his Father. Conversely, for them to refuse to be intimidated would mean that their death would pose for their adversaries the very decision that had been posed by Jesus' death.

The importance of these four statements should now be clear. They reveal the chief points at issue between the disciples and their adversaries. Who is the true God (the theological issue)? Who is the true Son (the Christological issue)? What is the true meaning of the cross? Why do disciples testify to God's glorification in that cross; why do their adversaries reject that witness? Why is the conflict inescapable? Finally, these statements spotlight John's concern to prepare his charismatic listeners for confronting the coming tests of their own vocation. Before exploring those tests in detail, let us examine two other ways in which the narrator identified the adversaries: his use of the terms "the Jews" and "the world."

John describes the opponents of Jesus as the rulers (four times), as Pharisees (nineteen times), and as high priests (twenty times). Often he links these groups together: Pharisees and priests (7:32, 45; 11:47, 57; 18:3) or Pharisees and rulers (7:48). Frequently, however, he simply dubs them "the Jews." In some cases this term does not indicate opposition to Jesus; it may refer to residents of Judea or to the common people, without any obvious animus. In at least twenty-three cases it refers, again without apparent prejudice, to the customs and the festivals of this people. Yet in almost forty cases it clearly reflects the bitter conflicts that erupted between John the Baptist and Jesus, on the one hand, and their opponents, on the other.

It is somewhat curious that the author should call his enemies "the Jews" when he was himself a Jewish Christian writing to Jewish Christians who were being expelled unwillingly from their home synagogues. What might have induced believing Jews to call their enemies the Jews? Obviously, they were not defining the term in a neutral or objective way. Nowhere in this Gospel are gentiles and Jews spoken of as two basic ethnic categories. How, then, does the author distinguish between Caiaphas and the disciples of Moses, on the one hand, and Jesus and his disciples, on the other, when all belonged to the same race and religion? In some passages a distinction is drawn between Israel and the Jews, with an implicit denial that the latter could rightly claim to be the former. The Jews "as a special term in John is clearly oriented to Judea-Jerusalem-the priesthood, and this in contrast to *Israel* and *laos* which denote the people of God, the children of God scattered throughout the world."[6] Disciples like Nathanael were "Israelites in whom is no guile [1:47]." Jesus is hailed as King of Israel, not king of the Jews (1:49; 12:13). It was not biological descent that made people truly the children of Abraham (8:39–44).[7] Such a pattern of thinking does not, however, fully explain the harsh polemical intent in the epithet "the Jews." How is the epithet to be explained?

The term had one advantage. Although Jesus attracted the hostility of separate groups among the leaders of his people, groups that were in fact at loggerheads with one another, their unanimity in opposing him invited the adoption of a single term. To say "the Jews" was a simple and economical way of including all opponents at once. An analogue may be found in Paul's letters. Although he was himself a Jew, whose love for his people never wavered despite extensive sufferings at their hands, he could write to Thessalonian Christians: "You suffered the same things from your own countrymen as they did from the Jews [sic], who killed both the Lord Jesus and the prophets, and drove us out [1 Thess. 2:14–15]."

Another factor may have been the tendency on the part of

these opponents to claim the term "the Jews" for themselves as a measure of self-confidence and as an implicit rejection of the right of Jesus to claim the term for himself. In fact, to exclude his followers from the synagogues embodied both this self-assurance and this rejection. It often happens that when the authority of religious leaders is challenged by a defiant minority, this becomes an almost automatic linguistic reaction: "We, not you, are Jews to whom the covenants and the promises belong. You have forfeited your right to use this name." (It is possible that Paul's adversaries in Romans 9—11 had been relying on this form of linguistic banishment.)

Still another explanation of the emotional heat stored up in John's use of this term was his prophetic resort to bitter, if sad, irony. The epithet is used most frequently in the Passion story, where the narrator intentionally discloses the depth of tragic self-deception. It is "the Jews" who say, "*We* have a law, and by that law he ought to die. . . . *We* have no king but Caesar [19:7, 15]." John underscores the blasphemy inherent in such statements and the self-righteousness of these servants of God (16:3). We may, accordingly, discern in John's use of this term an awareness of the infinite pathos disclosed in such confidence on the part of blind leaders who think they can see.

Behind this irony we may well perceive a much more serious theological conviction that comes to the surface in the words carved on the cross: "Jesus of Nazareth, the King of the Jews." The Jews themselves did their best to disclaim this title, but Pilate succeeded in frustrating their demands. This very altercation between the Roman and the Jews calls attention to the double meanings that John attached to both nouns: king, Jews. The title poses two questions: Who are truly the Jews? Of whom is Jesus king? To the narrator, the inscription was in fact true. It vindicated Jesus' royal power over his most intractable foes. The presence of "the Jews" at the coronation was essential if the cross were to demonstrate its power to take away "the sins of the world." It would be essential for the disciples to remember that very victory over the world when they faced a similar fate at the hands of the same foes.

The same irony and the same theological conviction are

31

embodied in John's use of the term "the world" to refer to these same enemies. As we have seen, the first few verses of chapter 16 identify those enemies with religious leaders who had sufficient authority to expel members from the synagogue and sufficient devotion to commit murder for God's sake. Throughout the Farewell Address John's thought centers on these leaders. They are pictured sharply in the previous paragraph (15:18–27), where John calls them "the world" no fewer than six times. "If they persecute me, they will persecute you [15:20]"; "All this they will do to you on my account, because they do not know him who sent me [15:21]," a verse that corresponds to 16:3. In this whole passage "the Jews" and "the world" are virtually inter-changeable terms (cf. also 16:8–11, 20, 28, 33). In some contexts and in some respects the world may be a more inclusive category, but in the context of *this* persecution the Jews *constitute* the world.

On at least one occasion the Jews returned the compliment with similar venom. When Jesus made his final entry into the holy city, and when a great crowd celebrated his arrival, the Pharisees said to one another: "You see that you can do nothing; look, the whole world [sic] has gone after him [12:19]." They were defending God's holy place against this intrusion by an untrained and irreligious mob. So when John speaks of them as "the world," he illustrates the pot's tendency to call the kettle black. Two communities were divided by two mutually exclusive concepts of what makes the world the world.

The Passion story represents the final collision between these two concepts of the world. Consider the innuendo in the conversation between Jesus and the high priest. Here there is no trial, with its presentation of charges; no summoning of witnes-ses; no defense; no rendering of a verdict. The Sanhedrin had already reached its verdict (11:47–53) and Jesus had already accepted it (12:27–33). The narrator rather focuses on a seem-ingly innocuous question about Jesus' disciples and about his teaching. We have already examined the answer insofar as it referred to his disciples; now for the answer about his teaching (18:20):

a I have spoken openly to the world;

b   I have always taught in synagogues and the temple,
b   where all Jews come together;
a   I have said nothing secretly.

These four lines form a chiasmus in which the *a* lines and the *b* lines are roughly parallel. All four lines appear to be statements of fact, so innocuous as to be accepted without quarrel. And yet they provoked an explosive effect on the officer of the court. He took Jesus' answer as a blatant insult to the high priest and an open challenge to his authority. Why should the narrator have located one of the least abrasive statements of Jesus at this dramatic moment? Or was that statement more abrasive than it seems? A careful examination of the chiastic structure may yield an answer. The lines marked *a* are synonymous "speaking openly" corresponds to "saying nothing secretly." Similarly, the lines marked *b* say much the same thing: The synagogues and temple are the places where all Jews gather. Most of the scenes in this Gospel occur in the synagogue on the sabbath or in the temple during a festival (and more in the latter than in the former).

Where, then, is the fuse that ignited the explosion? Only in one place. The answer given by Jesus equates the world in line *a* to the synagogues and temple in line *b*, those institutions that are under the administration of the Pharisees and the priests. It is they who constitute the world—an unthinkable insult. The officer who immediately struck Jesus recognized the insult. On his side the narrator treats the insult as both intended and true, as an accurate summary, in fact, of all previous episodes and as a prophetic anticipation of the events about to follow. In his answer at this strategic moment Jesus defined the world in precisely the same way as in 15:18—16:3. Here the priests were demonstrating their blindness (9:41) and Jesus was fulfilling his own prophetic mission to this very world. *Here* is the world.[8]

In Jesus' conversation with Pilate the same location is assigned to the world. Now Pilate, as neutral interlocutor, asks questions that focus the readers' attention on three matters: Jesus as king of the Jews, the Jews as rejecting their king, the character of the world as disclosed by that rejection. The dialogue in 18:33–37 answers those questions.

PILATE:	Are you king of the Jews?
JESUS:	Do you say this of your own accord, or did others say it to you about me?
PILATE:	Am I a Jew? Your own nation and the chief priests have handed you over to me; what have you done?
JESUS:	*a* My kingship is not of this world;
	b if my kingship were of this world, my servants would fight,
	c that I might not be handed over to the Jews;
	d but my kingship is not from the world.
PILATE:	So you are a king?
JESUS:	You say that I am a king.
	For this I was born,
	and for this I have come into the world,
	to bear witness to the truth.

In this interchange the world is mentioned four times, surely an index of its importance. In all four cases Jesus' kingship is contrasted with the world; the two are seen to be mutually exclusive. In a sense they are the ultimate antagonists, and between them a final battle is being fought. By the same token, Jesus' answer forges a strong bond between the Jews and the world, a bond so close that the two seem to be interchangeable. The world is not a vague, general blur but a specific group of people; not an irreligious group but a superreligious one: "your own nation and the chief priests." Jesus uses three alternate ways of defining the same conflict: those who fight vs. those who do not fight; the world vs. the kingdom; the Jews vs. the witness to the truth.

To associate the Jews with the world says something about the Jews; their violent rejection of their king reveals the tragic irony of their self-deception. It says something about the world; it is to be located wherever this illusion is to be found. As a prophetic witness to the truth, this king aims at destroying that self-deception, but he (and his servants) can do that only by coming "into the world" and there renouncing the use of violence. It is not surprising that Pilate disqualified himself from judging that issue.[9]

We have now examined virtually every use of the term "the world" in the last nine chapters of the Gospel and have found everywhere this close association with Jesus' adversaries, the Pharisees and the high priests. The question arises whether the same association appears in the first twelve chapters. We cannot survey all relevant texts, but such passages as 3:1–21; 7:1–7; and 9:18–41 yield a positive answer. Thus the search for an identification of the adversaries of Jesus has led us from the more objective and empirical categories (rulers, priests, Pharisees) to a more inclusive category (Jews), and then to a highly polemic category (the world), with its ironic connotations of darkness, blindness, self-deception, and violence, placed at the command of self-righteousness, both personal and institutional. So whenever we encounter any of these categories in reading this document, we should reckon with their assigned role as enemies of the King of Israel. We should also reckon with them as continuing to be the adversaries of John's readers, whether believers or their charismatic leaders.

One more category, equally polemic, should be mentioned. To introduce it we may observe that the equation between the Jews and the world falls short of being absolute. In such texts as the following John draws a distinction between the two. Notice this parallel couplet: "You are from below, I am from above; you are of this world, I am not of this world [8:23]." Here the conflict between Jesus and his adversaries is not minimized, but their blindness and violence is traced to a hidden source, indicated by the significant prepositions from and of. "This world" is their place of origin, their habitat. Their hostility can be understood only when it is traced to this hidden source, that is, a source hidden from the blind but disclosed to the eye of the prophet. Another image for conveying this source of the Jews' hostility is to speak of them as children of the devil. In doing what the devil does, they act as his offspring (8:44). This says something about the Jews: In the action in which they are confident of serving God they are actually serving the devil (16:2). Violence is a measure of their self-deception. This also says something about the devil: As the ruler of "this world" he makes religious rulers his puppets, using his lies to make them liars. "Only the devil could have thought up all the deceits and guises under which death masquerades."[10] John recognizes him as the ultimate enemy whom Jesus must defeat.

The hour marks the final conflict between two kings and signals "the judgment of this world," when "the ruler of this world" is expelled (12:31). That hour makes clear the lines of conflict, the stakes being won and lost, the sources of power and the character of the strategies used by the two armies. The story is shaped to meet the needs of John's readers during the period prophesied by Jesus. An understanding of the one story carries over to the later stories as well, for if readers understand the devil's wiles, they will understand the power of Jesus' prayer to protect them from those wiles. And they will welcome the gift of the Paraclete with its power to convince the world that its former ruler has already been judged (16:11).

Chapter IV

THE OBJECTIVES

Once you invoked any kind of revelation—
however hallowed by tradition—you were
committed to an ultimate insanity.[1]

Only strong motives can account for the work involved in composing any document, ancient or modern. In the case of the Gospel of John it has often been assumed that such motivation centered in the finer points of doctrine about Jesus. I am convinced that this assumption is faulty. We should rather look for the strongest motives to arise from the difficulties encountered by a missionary church. In this chapter we will examine, in a preliminary way, some of those difficulties.

We have now studied the role adopted by the narrator as he responded to the Spirit of truth that had been given by the victorious Lord to his disciples and to their successors. We have identified his first audience as being composed of two groups: men and women who, in accepting Jesus as God's son, had received rebirth through the Spirit; men and women whom the Lord had appointed as shepherds of his flock. These two groups quite naturally identified themselves with the believers and the disciples in John's stories. Of these two groups, the narrator, perhaps because of his own charisma, was more keenly aware of the needs of the second.

We have also observed how completely the narrator pictured the adversaries of Jesus as "the Jews" who had succeeded in their conspiracy against Jesus. Moreover, the narrator pictured the disciples as facing the same adversaries and paying the same price for victory in their hour as Jesus had paid in his. Pictures of the present were screened through memories of the past in such a way as to make those two *hours* the brackets within which John's community lived, looking back to the hour of Jesus and ahead to their own hour. Those who "take up temporary residence" in that community must be able to imagine the whole range of needs faced by its members, whether followers or leaders. The better we can imagine those needs, the more readily we will recover the deeper motives of the author.

Sheep and shepherds alike were recipients of the gift of the Spirit; they had committed themselves to obey the risen Lord. Although bound together by the same loyalty, the two groups were subject to somewhat different hazards. We can therefore distinguish between the dominant needs of the two groups. The needs of believers appear to be foremost in the episodes of chapters 2—12; the trials of the disciples dominate the dialogues of chapters 13—17. We will examine the two sections in that order.

The story of Nicodemus provides a mirror reflecting the range of attitudes that the narrator wanted believers to adopt toward themselves and their opponents. Our edition of the story, which probably first circulated in oral form, begins at 2:23, in Jerusalem at the Passover, a strategic place and time. Here it is said for the first time that many believed in his name, but it is also said that Jesus did not entrust himself to these believers. In reading this, how would later believers react? Would they readily identify themselves with those first Passover believers? Would the story help them to detect points in which they did not as yet believe? Would the story lead them to say, "Does Jesus, who knows what is in us, trust our confessions of faith in him?" Would they find in Jesus' conversation with Nicodemus a pattern that their own later conversations might follow? How should they deal with potential converts who came to them "by night"?

The story allows us to discern some of the basic attitudes of the narrator. For example, he saw a sharp contrast between Nicodemus' admiration for Jesus and such basic belief as would have signaled eternal life. The narrator was convinced that, although rebirth through the Spirit was as yet impossible for Nicodemus as a teacher of Israel, such rebirth was open to every Israelite. Rebirth was, in fact, a fulfillment of prophecies imbedded in the work of Moses and in Israel's deliverance from slavery (3:14). The impasse between believers and Nicodemus at this first Passover would be present whenever later believers addressed Nicodemus' successors: "We bear witness to what we have seen." The narrator wanted readers to realize that this confession must be given even in the face of almost certain rejection: "You do not receive our testimony [3:11]" (the plurals in this verse, *you* and *our,* represent a shift away from the original dialogue between two individuals). Like his readers, John could look back on an event, the ascent of the Son of man into heaven (3:13), which Nicodemus' successors did not know had happened. So when we read this story as a transcript of continuing relationships between believers and the rulers of Israel, we are able to detect various needs on the part of John and his readers, even though our descriptions of those needs remain provisional.

We can be confident of the presence of such needs as these: Believers needed to prove themselves worthy of Jesus' trust (2:24). This involved much more than such admiration as Jesus' signs had evoked on the part of Nicodemus. It also involved accepting the alienation from the rulers of Israel that was produced by any rebirth through the Spirit. Believers were required to respect their adversaries without trying to appease them, giving their testimonies to them without fear or favor. They must rely on the guidance by the Spirit, even though their adversaries could not see "whence it comes and whither it goes [3:8]." They must assert that their new community is an authentic fulfillment of the prophecy of Moses and of God's promises to Israel.

For us to read this episode as an encounter between Jesus and Nicodemus is entirely natural. I am convinced, however, that this episode becomes much more illuminating when read as a major segment of John's conversation with his readers. In that context the following paragraph expresses in rich detail their shared testimony to the successors of Nicodemus.

God so loved the world that he gave his only Son, that whoever believes in him should not perish but have eternal life. For God sent the Son into the world, not to condemn the world, but that the world might be saved through him. He who believes in him is not condemned; he who does not believe is condemned already, because he has not believed

39

in the name of the only Son of God. And this is the judgment, that the light has come into the world, and men loved darkness rather than light, because their deeds were evil. For everyone who does evil hates the light, and does not come to the light, lest his deeds be exposed. But whoever does what is true comes to the light, that it may be clearly seen that his deeds have been wrought in God [3:16–21].

It is the narrator who speaks here with the authority of the Spirit, the authority of a prophet to whom God's love has been revealed. He is looking back on the story he is telling (God *gave,* God *sent,* the light *has come*) and he is looking at a present period in which crucial decisions are being made, choices of believing and hating and loving and living. In that present period he is speaking to a community of believers about the world, about God's actions and attitudes toward it, and about that world's hatred of the light and its love for darkness.

This is the adversarial world that we analyzed in chapter III. Now it is true that the famous 3:16 is not often placed in that context; but I am confident that the narrator had that very world in his mind. This paragraph is his final comment on this first scene in the drama of Nicodemus (we will look at the second and third scenes later), an unbelieving ruler of the Jews who at first found the requirement of rebirth too fantastic to accept. Jesus' ironic question, "Are you a teacher of Israel [3:10]?" implies that although Nicodemus was to be honored as a teacher, he nevertheless lacked the qualifications for understanding the work of the Spirit. In this summary by the narrator, Nicodemus is the only person on the stage to represent the world to whom God has sent this Son. The words "not to condemn the world" imply that this world merits condemnation; it is in fact the same world that is so graphically pictured in 15:18—16:3.

The whole paragraph stresses the condemnation under which this world stands because of its hatred of the light and its love for darkness, both exemplified by its evil deeds in rejecting the Son and in continued refusal to believe in his name. The narrator announces God's final judgment on that world. But he is even more concerned to define precisely how that judgment has been executed. "This is the judgment"—in that blunt declaration the world's perceptions of reality have been turned upside down. The judgment has been executed in God's love for the world, in the gift of the Son to the world. The world's condemnation and salvation operate simultaneously through the light that splits the darkness, the love that provokes the hatred. To believe is to believe in the Son through whom this world that hates him is judged and loved. In the death of his Son the Father offers life *to his enemies.* This is the "ultimate insanity" of the revelation that this narrator is trying to convey to his readers. To believe in that insanity is what requires a rebirth through the Spirit. The hostile world *is* the beloved world; the beloved world *is* the hostile world. Accordingly, the Nicodemus story raises this question for every self-styled believer:

1. Are you a person to whom Jesus can trust himself? (2:24). For you to believe in the signs is wholly inadequate, for Nicodemus was capable of that.
2. You must be willing to come to Jesus by day, boldly confessing even to the synagogue rulers that their victim, in being crucified, was like the serpent that Moses lifted up in the wilderness.
3. You must love those enemies in the same way and to the same extent as Jesus.

That in essence is the implicit command as relayed by the text. The concluding sentence brings this command to the surface. By coming to the light, believers must do what is true so that their adversaries may be able to see that their deeds "have been wrought in God [3:21]."

When we allow the dilemmas of the mission to define the thrust of the believers' confession, the familiar verses take on an ominous relevance:

God loved his deadly enemies so much that he gave his only Son to be crucified by them, so that those enemies who come to believe in him should not perish but have eternal life. The Father sent the Son to the Jews who rejected him, not in order to condemn them but in order to save them through him [3:16, paraphrased].

Believing entails sharing in that mission. This is surely why Jesus did not entrust himself to believers, why so many believers were guilty of so many misunderstandings, why only a rebirth through the Spirit could engender belief, and why the narrator, in addressing readers who already believed, could say, "These are written that you may believe . . . and that believing you may have life in his name [20:31]."

We are right, then, in concluding that a major motive in the composition of the Gospel was to instill belief among the believing, but that conclusion is correct only when we recapture all the aspects of the mission that could undermine belief. For example, many episodes make it clear that fear, rather than unbelief, is the genuine antithesis of believing. In these episodes, believers kept their faith secret, out of fear of the Jews. Other episodes picture belief as momentary and ephemeral. And that was not strange, because the Jews kept all who were baptized under strict surveillance (3:22–26). The blind man discovered, with his parents, the hazards of being healed (9:22, 34). After Lazarus was raised from the dead his life was placed in the same jeopardy as that of Jesus (12:10f.). The narrator does not minimize the dangers. He does, however, counter any suggestion of futility or despair. Witnessing is able to produce belief even among one-time enemies. "Many even of the authorities believed in him, but for fear of the Pharisees they did not confess it, lest they should be put out of the synagogue: for they loved the praise of men more than the praise of God [12:42–43]." Belief in Jesus aroused enmity; enmity aroused fear; fear silenced testimony; yet testimony awakened belief. A victory over fear became a major objective of the narrator, for he realized that such fear was absolutely incompatible with true belief in the Crucified. The test of true belief was to share in God's love for those very enemies.

Now we turn to an examination of John's objectives for the shepherd-successors of the disciples. Just as the inclusive goal for the sheep was a full comprehension and acceptance of Jesus' mission to the world, so the inclusive goal for the shepherds was the uninhibited pursuit of the same mission. As the narrator proceeds with the conversation between Jesus and the chosen recipients of the Spirit, "an amazing correlation begins to take shape: the character and function of Jesus is identical with the character and function of the followers."[2] Disciples were commanded to emulate his actions (e.g., washing feet), to keep his word (i.e., his commands), to do his works and even greater works, and to exercise his authority to retain or to forgive sins. Like him, they would be rejected and persecuted by the same antagonists and would be denied any immunity or privilege. The Farewell Address is an unqualified declaration of the virtual identity of the two missions or, better, of the unbroken continuity of the same mission under the guidance of the Paraclete, which John viewed as Jesus' alter ego. Missiology and martyrology become intrinsically inseparable. And when we ask why he should have stressed the radical rigor that the mission placed on the shepherds, the conjecture is immediately at hand: Those shepherds needed such a reminder because they were inclined to read the terms of their own assignments in a less demanding and daunting form. This is surely why the narrator normally pictures the disciples as misunderstanding those terms; they were too timorous to accept them (at least until after the crucifixion).

One reason for their hesitations is certainly the opposition of "the world." Because the charismatic leaders of the church would bear the brunt of that world's brutality, it would be their falling away that would be most disastrous to their cause. Only a continued victory over fear of social ostracism and death could give them the necessary stamina to carry out their assignments. It is the power of such fear that explains the infrastructure of the Farewell Address. That power reaches its climax in the behavior of the disciples during the arrest and trial of Jesus. In his speech, in his prayer, and in his reactions to Judas, to Caiaphas, and to Pilate, Jesus' own courage casts a harsh light on the craven anxieties of his chosen messengers. Yet at the same time he entrusts his cause to them with an assurance that they could and would win a victory over those very anxieties. And behind this portrait of Jesus we may discern the hand of the painter. In the prayer of intercession, two intercessors are praying. When Jesus said, "I have said all this to keep you from falling away," we are entitled to overhear another voice: "I have *written* all this to keep you from falling away." As a whole, the Gospel becomes a powerful appeal to courage (*parrhesia,* 7:26; 10:24; 16:25; 18:20).

Because the disciples' panic was grounded in self-concern, one way of fighting it was to encourage a substitute concern, concern for the flock that Jesus had placed under the care of

Peter and his colleagues. The strength of fears is always measurable in terms of the strength of loyalties. The shepherd who gives priority to self becomes a hired servant and not a shepherd; only the shepherd who gives priority to the flock can be accepted as a surrogate for the good shepherd (10:12–13). Thus Peter's impetuous assertion of loyalty to Jesus (13:36–38), his swordplay in the Garden, his evasive maneuvers in the court of the high priest, and his final dialogue with Jesus—all these episodes are skillfully presented with an eye to Peter's successors. It would be in the feeding of Jesus' sheep that they, like Peter, would overcome their instincts for self-preservation.

Just as one of the objectives of persecutors is to fragment the community under attack, one objective of leaders must be the protection of the community's unity. Here and there wolves may separate a lamb from the flock, but wolves find it more effective if they can create dissension among the shepherds. And that often happens when some of those shepherds adopt policies of silence or compromise, and their colleagues compensate for their betrayal by exaggerating the demand for self-sacrifice. The ensuing debate can demoralize the entire community. It is possible to sense such a danger lying behind the recurrent commands to love one another and behind the prayer "that all may be one." The command and the prayer are needed because those virtues are in short supply and because such disputes destroy the mission's chance for success.

Sometimes the erosion of unity results from inner tensions created by the dynamics of divine revelation. An outburst of charismatic gifts almost always releases tremendous centrifugal forces. A group of prophets often discovers that the winds of the Spirit are as turbulent as a tornado. The boundary between true prophecy and false prophecy becomes hard to determine. And when priority is given to the role of prophecy, many members of the community will seek that role, and a conflict of interest develops. Personal prestige and power become confused with guidance by the Spirit; the result: competition among the prophets as leaders of the church. Such competition may well lie behind the insistent demands of Jesus that love for him be measured by readiness to die for one another. The Farewell Address insists that only those who keep his commands can claim to love him or can claim that they have received the Spirit from his Father (cf. below, chapter VI). Such insistence is most needed when most neglected.

Leaders of a religious community that is subject to intense hostility from specific individuals often find it virtually impossible to distinguish those immediate enemies from their ultimate enemy. We have seen that Jesus, according to the Gospel, separated "the world" from "the ruler of the world," and that his central objective was victory over that ruler. In identifying the work of the charismatic leaders as a continuation of the work of Jesus, the narrator wanted to convey an awareness of their ultimate enemy, who could be overcome only by use of the same weapon as Jesus had used. He wanted to alert them to the deceptive designs of "the evil one" (17:15), who is the source of all temptations, all misunderstandings, all self-deceptions. Human enemies could kill, but the fear of death was the work of the devil, so that victory over that fear was victory over the ultimate enemy. It is this understanding of the ultimate enemy that marks shepherds as candidates for martyrdom. In fact, the Farewell Address can be read as a suicide pact between the Good Shepherd and his undershepherds. In the hour of martyrdom many objectives converged: a victory over the devil, a love for God and for the Son, a love for the one flock, a love for the Jews, the liberation of those enemies from their illusions of serving God, the discovery by the world that God had sent Jesus (17:21, 23).

The ultimate issue was whether or not Jesus was the true revealer and whether or not his revelation was the truth. What the disciples accepted as true revelation their enemies rejected as an ultimate insanity. Yet the Gospel makes it clear that the God-given task of the disciples was to bring the light of the world into the world of the blind. Only by such a shining would their mission find completion: coming from God through Jesus, through the Paraclete, through the disciples, through their charismatic successors, it moved into the world that God loved. The narrator believed that when charismatic leaders in the churches grasped fully the logistics of this war against "the evil one," they would in truth be able to continue the mission of Jesus.

The mission required daily contacts with individual unbelieving Jews and with specific authorities in the synagogues and in the temple. The narrator was interested in providing guidance on how to carry on discussions with these people. Just as more than half the Gospel was devoted to describing Jesus' debates before his hour had come, so the narrator anticipated a similar period of work before the advent of their hour. This suggests that we may well read the early chapters of John as providing materials that would be useful to Jesus' delegates when they debated with their opponents. They must understand the harvest field. They must take full account of the stance of their adversaries as disciples of Moses (9:28) who placed their hope in Moses (5:45) and believed that the decisive revelation of God had been through that prophet (9:29). Those opponents were adept in interpreting the scriptures (5:38) and devout in obeying God's commands to keep the sabbath holy. Disciples of Jesus must not denigrate the degree to which their adversaries were sincere in denying that Jesus was a prophet like Moses and greater than Abraham.[3] So the earlier debates between Jesus and Jewish leaders became object lessons in how charismatic leaders in John's day should carry on their own debates. Various passages make it clear that John

> is undoubtedly attempting to provide the members of the Johannine communities with arguments with which they can defend themselves in the debate with the synagogue and to enable them within their own circles to think through the implications of the position they have adopted.[4]

Most, if not all, of the friction points between Jesus and the Pharisees probably continued to be sources of friction for the Johannine community. The debates, of course, continued on different levels. One level was that of daily behavior, such as the observance of sabbath regulations, participation in the annual festivals, worship in the temple, and fellowship with Samaritans and gentiles. Another level was controversy over the role of Jesus. J. Louis Martyn sees this controversy as centering in three matters: "the technical question of Jesus' messiahship; the correct interpretation of his signs; the relationship between him and the towering-figure of Judaism, Moses."[5] Every term used to describe Jesus' work by his followers was contested by their adversaries: messiah, prophet, king, judge, shepherd, way, word, truth, light, life. And each contest called for the charismatic leaders of the church to clarify the meaning of the Christian claim, both for believers and for unbelievers. Still a deeper level of conflict stemmed from the role of the Jews in the death of Jesus, for this involved either an ultimate guilt or an ultimate approval. Could they claim credit with God for their efforts to serve him or were they guilty of fighting against him (16:2)? For the narrator, all issues centered in the cross.[6] Did it vindicate or invalidate Christian allegiance to Jesus as one who "reigns from the cross"?[7] And for those who received the Paraclete, the issue was resolved by viewing the whole story of Jesus vs. the Jews as a revelation of the lawsuit that had been held in the heavenly courtroom, God vs. Satan. George B. Caird has described what happened when Satan lost his case in that court.

> The case is not closed, for the world does not know that its case is lost. . . . The witness passes to the apostles and the Advocate, the Spirit of truth (15:26, 27). . . . The function of the Advocate is to convince the world that it has been wrong in bringing Jesus to trial and execution, wrong about the meaning of sin, wrong about the meaning of righteousness, wrong about the meaning of judgment. (16:8–11)[8]

It was the conviction of the narrator that the leaders in his churches would find the guidance of the Advocate indispensable; the Gospel is his way of conveying that same conviction.

Chapter V

THE TIME FRAME

It is more dangerous to tread on the corns
of a live giant than to cut off the head of
a dead one; but it is more useful and better fun.[1]

To take up temporary residence in the Johannine community requires some answers, however tentative, to questions of where to locate the community in space and time. Yet scholars find it impossible to agree on such answers. On the map of the ancient world various places have been chosen—the land of Israel, the Jewish Diaspora, the Hellenistic world. My own studies have pointed increasingly in the direction chosen by W.H. Brownlee: "Wherever else the Evangelist preached, the substance of his message seems to have been worked out in the living context of the varied population of the land of Israel."[2] We have seen that "the Jews" were the only representatives of "the world" to which Jesus sent his disciples on their hazardous mission. They are the only enemies pictured in the Gospel. In this respect "there are many indications of a situation similar to that underlying the first chapters in Acts."[3]

Scholars choose an even wider range of points on the time line—from A.D. 50 to almost 150. It used to be the fashion to assign the writing to the early part of the second century; more recently the greater favorite is a date at the end of the first century. Only a small minority defends a date during the first generation of Christian history, before the disastrous war with Rome left Jerusalem destroyed and the temple in rubble. For my part, I find within the Gospel no clear evidence of knowledge of that war and, indeed, much evidence that the war lay in the future. The only date that is clearly required by the internal evidence is some time after the deaths of Peter and the beloved disciple, which are mentioned in chapter 21.

My purpose in this book precludes a full marshaling of the evidence for and against this early dating. However, because many scholars will reject my interpretation of the Gospel as made impossible by their conviction of a later date, I must indicate some of my reasons for favoring the prewar dating. (Readers who are unconcerned by this problem may choose to skip this chapter.) I rely almost entirely on internal evidence, and I think that this evidence favors the conclusion that the narrator was a Jerusalemite who was dealing with "the religious, political, and geographical conditions of Palestine and Jerusalem prior to the war of 66–70 A.D."[4] Let me mention briefly the data that have led me to this conclusion.

• The story as a whole deals with Jesus' mission to the Jews, and predominantly to the Jews in Judea and Jerusalem. Only when the hour of Jesus' death comes near is the presence of Greeks (perhaps Hellenistic Jews) mentioned. Only the authorities in Jerusalem wielded the powers indicated in the Gospel, and it is to them that Jesus sent his disciples for work after his death.

• The whole range of vocabulary and imagery was indigenous to Jewish culture during this period and would have been readily understood by Jewish-Christian readers.

• The reliance on scriptural allusions (manna, vine, fig tree, harvest, water) and the methods of interpreting scripture were entirely congruent with patterns of thought in the Jewish homeland.[5]

• Many segments of the Gospel reflect an origin in worship. The perspectives and patterns are those indigenous to Jewish worship or to Christian forms derived from synagogue and temple.[6]

• Various episodes are presented in such a way as to presuppose the prewar status of Jerusalem and the temple. For example, the Samaritan woman says to Jesus: "You say that in Jerusalem *is* the place where men ought to worship [4:20]." Such a statement would have lost its force after the temple lay in shambles. In the same story Jesus' way of linking Gerizim to Jerusalem implies that both mountains were still accessible to worship in John's day as well (4:20). There are similar implications in the narrator's comment: "There *is* in Jerusalem by the Sheep Gate a pool [5:2]." Note too that the phrase "beyond the Jordan" as a way of referring to the area *east* of the river implies a stance *west* of the river (1:28; 3:26; 10:40).

• It is a striking fact that the narrator locates more incidents in the temple than in any other single place (the Synoptics prefer the synagogues of Galilee). This tendency is inexplicable if, at the time of writing, the temple was no longer the place "where all Jews come together [18:20]." After the destruction of the temple the significance of the synagogue increased rapidly, but of this development there is no trace in John.

• Although the destruction of the temple marked the virtual end of the authority of the chief priests, there is in John no hint of a disruption in their prestige and power; rather, it is assumed that they will continue in their murderous way at least until "the hour" of the disciples.

• What is true of temple and priesthood is true also of the annual festivals that were celebrated in the temple until its desecration. Jesus' visits to Jerusalem often coincided with these festivals. Their traditional symbolism (the exodus, manna, water, light, the giving of the Law) permeates the Johannine interpretations of those visits. No hint is given that the site of those celebrations had shifted before the Gospel was written. In fact, many of the subtler nuances in those narratives would have become obsolete and less intelligible after such a shift.*

• As an illustration, we may take the account of Jesus' first trip to the temple at the Passover. The narrator's setting for the incident presupposes that the temple was still being used for worship. More even than this: The temple is still under con-

---

*Matthias Rissi believes that the journeys of Jesus to Jerusalem provided the basic pattern on which the Gospel was organized. Not only do his journeys lead there, but they also coincide with the annual festivals. In this city his Father's house is located, here his Father's glory will be manifested. All this would become meaningless after the city lay in ruins.[7]

struction. After its destruction there would have been less significance accorded to Jesus' zeal for his Father's house. There would have been no sacrificial animals to expel and no money changers. The abrasive protest against commercialization and desecration that Jesus leveled at the authorities would have lost most of its power to arouse his enemies. Notice too how the thrust of his prophetic prediction would have been altered. When the Jews asked him for a sign, he answered:

"Destroy this temple, and in three days I will raise it up." The Jews then said, "It has taken forty-six years to build this temple, and will you raise it up in three days?" But he spoke of the temple of his body. When therefore he was raised from the dead, his disciples remembered that he had said this; and they believed the scripture and the word which Jesus had spoken [2:19–22].

This whole dialogue hinges on the hypothetical destruction of two temples. It assumes not only that the buildings in Jerusalem are still standing but also that those buildings are indestructible. After the Romans had proved otherwise, the protest of "the Jews" would have become almost unintelligible. To be sure, Jesus and John had in mind a different temple, but the character of that temple is underscored by its contrast to the place of worship in Jerusalem. The antithesis on which the thought is based would have lost much of its cogency in the absence of the buildings themselves. Rubble hardly provides an adequate foil for the temple of Jesus' body. Also observe the implications of the last sentence. It shows that the narrator had shaped his understanding of the incident to accord with later developments after the resurrection, when Jesus' prediction about his body had been fulfilled. But there is no similar editorial change to bring the story into conformity with the situation after the Romans had left the buildings in ruins, after empirical events had themselves proved any confidence in the temple's indestructibility illusory. In short, the editorial work reflects the period before the war, not the period after that war.

• I call attention also to another strategic dialogue that the war would have made both otiose and innocuous. As the episode in chapter 2 marked the first open battle between Jesus and "the

Jews," this episode marked the last such battle, because here the Sanhedrin arrived at its decision to put Jesus to death. It made this decision under extreme pressure—pressure attributed to the fact that "many of the Jews believed in him [11:45]." In their debate, "the chief priests and the Pharisees" considered how to meet the emergency.

> "If we let him go on thus, everyone will believe in him, and the Romans will come and destroy both our holy place and our nation." But one of them, Caiaphas, who was high priest that year, said to them, "You know nothing at all; you do not understand that it is expedient for you that one man should die for the people, and that the whole nation should not perish." He did not say this of his own accord, but being high priest that year he prophesied that Jesus should die for the nation, and not for the nation only, but to gather into one the children of God who are scattered abroad [11:48–52].

Three futures are sketched in this passage: the future provoked by the fear of the group, the future anticipated by the prophet Caiaphas, and the future (the death of Jesus) to which the narrator now looked back. None of these three has place for any reference to the war of 66–70. The first two clearly exclude knowledge of that war. Consider the first future. In that war the Romans did come and did destroy "both our holy place and our nation." But would the narrator have described the fear of the Council in those precise terms if that disaster had already taken place and if it had not had the slightest connection with the work of Jesus that had been completed forty years earlier? It is highly doubtful. Similar doubts apply to Caiaphas' prophecy, which focused simultaneously on the death of one man and the salvation of the nation. Responsive to Caiaphas' plea, the Sanhedrin voted the death of this one man in order to save the nation; but the plan misfired. The execution did nothing whatever to prevent the nation from perishing. The events of 66–70 demonstrated the failure of Caiaphas' prediction, but the narrator does not comment on that failure, which is strange if he had been writing after that date. When one considers how often the narrator interpreted other predictions in the light of subsequent events, it is surprising that he did not reinterpret Caiaphas' prophecy in the light of the Roman catastrophe. Instead, John was content to stress the twin facts that Jesus actually did die for the people (although in a sense different from the high priest's intention), and that his death kept the nation from perishing (again, in a different sense). In a word, although this whole summary of the issues centers in the salvation of the nation, not the slightest reference is made to the disasters that befell that nation, the temple, and the priesthood. If the narrator was writing after those disasters, it is hard to explain the absence of any trace of them.*

In this connection it is important to observe that the narrator approves Caiaphas' announcement that Jesus would die *for Israel.* As C.H. Dodd noted, this approval must be traced to "a Jewish Christian circle still acutely conscious of its solidarity with 'the commonwealth of Israel.'"[9] In addition, the saying reflects a commitment on the narrator's part to continue the same sacrificial ministry to the same "nation." Even more than this, the evaluation of the office of the high priest as potentially prophetic could only be expected from "an early Palestinian Jewish Christianity still within the body of the Jewish nation, and sharing in general its beliefs and religious attitudes."[10]

• J.A.T. Robinson has called attention to the shift in Jewish attitudes toward the Romans that the war evoked. The story of Jesus shows that under the rule of Pilate "the relations with Rome are still courteous and sycophantic to the point of irony."[11] But after the war that degree of irony would have lost its credibility. The war would have made it unthinkable for a Christian writer to attribute to the Jews that horrible accusation, "We have no king but Caesar [19:15; cf. 19:12]." And even bitter enemies of Jesus would hardly have used the charge against him that he sets himself against Caesar. After the war such a charge would have become a mark to his credit with other Jews. So too before

---

*There is some evidence that after the destruction of Jerusalem some Jewish-Christians viewed the event as divine punishment on the Jews for their rejection of the Messiah; of that attitude there is not the slightest trace in this Gospel.[8]

the war writers could picture the Roman governor as submitting to the demands of the priests out of fear of their power—but not afterward!

• The war produced major changes in Jewish religious life and its institutional expressions. Among these changes perhaps the most important was the shift in the center of authority from the priesthood in Jerusalem to the rabbinical school at Jamnia. Of this shift I find no convincing evidence in the Gospel. This statement calls for some discussion, for it is precisely such evidence that impels many scholars to date the Gospel after the Jamnia school had been established and after its authority over synagogue procedures had become widely recognized. The controverted evidence is located primarily in the three texts in John that refer to Christian believers being excommunicated from the synagogues (9:22; 12:42; 16:2). How are these texts to be interpreted?

In his influential study of the Gospel, J. Louis Martyn traces the policy of excommunication to an authoritative action first taken by the rabbis at Jamnia.[12] Martyn argues that the term used by John *(aposynagogos)* represents formal official action, based on an established policy adopted by a central authority.[13] He links this policy to the publication of a ban on heretics that was included in the Eighteen Benedictions, a step that could have been taken only by the Jamnia academy and probably not before A.D. 80. This ban made the confession of faith in Jesus as the Messiah incompatible with synagogue membership; the ban therefore produced a final, official separation of the church from the synagogue. Martyn distinguishes this formal, official, and general exclusion from earlier, localized, and spontaneous actions in which believers in Christ became victims of violence in synagogue brawls. For example, Paul's efforts in persecuting followers of Christ (Galatians 1:13; Philippians 3:6) in Jerusalem and Damascus were examples of internal policing and not of official expulsions, even though Paul acknowledged that he was trying to destroy the church. And when, after his conversion, Paul suffered from similar violence he was not being declared *aposynagogos.* Although on five occasions he received the Jewish penalty of thirty-nine lashes and on at least one occasion was stoned, a normally fatal penalty (2 Corinthians 11:24–25), there is no evidence that Paul was ever excommunicated. I believe that this interpretation rests too heavily on the conjectured history of one word, *aposynagogos*, ignoring its virtual equivalence to other terms, current in the first generation, to describe exclusion (e.g., *ekballo*, 9:34–35, and its subtle contrast to the action of Jesus in 6:37; 12:31). The interpretation also rests heavily on the assumption that the action of excommunication did not exist until it was legitimized in a formal way. Official procedures often lag far behind unofficial practice. Surely the act of stoning deviants must be viewed as tantamount to exclusion from the synagogue. In citing 16:2, Martyn[14] stops with the reference to expulsion from the synagogue and does not comment on v. 2*b*, with its reference to murder; I find v. 2*b* a far more significant index of date than v. 2*a*. There can be no doubt that in the first decades of the church Jewish authorities were directly responsible for assassinating their opponents as false prophets and teachers (Jesus, Stephen, Peter, James, Paul are only the known cases). Given the evidence of such violent animosities during those earliest decades, we may be confident that local decisions to exclude believers from synagogues were quickly and spontaneously taken, without waiting for formal authorization from any central rabbinic body. At any rate, it is hard for me to visualize a form of exclusion more drastic than crucifixion or stoning. This is why, in my judgment, texts like 16:1–3 are better mirrors of the situation in Judea before A.D. 66 than of a more generalized situation in Galilee or Syria after A.D. 80.

Admittedly, however, most scholars have adopted the latter dating. And it must also be admitted that among the editorial comments in the Gospel, a number seem to imply an audience of non-Jews outside the area of the Judean heartland. I cite a few instances. The origin of scripture quotations is often specified ("as the prophet Isaiah said") despite the fact that Jewish Christians would already know the source. Other facts are mentioned that would have been common knowledge to Jews in Judea: "Jews had no dealings with Samaritans [4:9]." Residents of Jerusalem would have had no need to be told that Bethany was near Jerusalem (11:18) or that "there *is* in Jerusalem . . . a pool . . . called Beth-zatha [5:2]." They would already have been familiar with the times of the festivals and would not need the narrator's note that the feast of the Dedication came in the winter (10:22–23). Nor would they have needed to have the meaning of Hebrew or Aramaic terms spelled out (20:16) or the burial customs of the Jews explained (19:40). It is not easy to harmonize all these data with the provenance we have adopted.

Similar difficulties, however, emerge on *any* choice of a single time frame for the entire Gospel. Although it is the consensus that the Gospel was intended primarily for Christian readers, many of the editor's comments would have been unnecessary for them. They already knew that Judas had been one of the twelve and that Jesus had raised Lazarus, who had been a resident of Bethany. They knew well what kind of death Jesus had died. They did not need Nicodemus identified, nor were they unaware of Peter's martyrdom. Yet data of this sort do not disprove a Christian readership. Comments like these functioned not simply to relay hitherto unknown information but also to furnish tags of recognition, reminders that the saga of revelation and redemption had involved well-known persons and familiar surroundings near at hand.

The lack of scholarly consensus with regard to the provenance of John makes one thing clear: No single setting in space and time can explain all the data within the Gospel. Because of this fact, no one can speak with certainty about its origins. Perhaps this is due to the probability that the Gospel began its life not as a single document, composed at one place and time, but as a collection of stories and conversations that had emerged at different places and times, each of which had a separate history (oral and/or written) before this narrator collected, edited, and published them in a single connected story.[15]

The difficulties of dating this document are such that no interpreter can claim certainty. Recognizing those difficulties and disclaiming undue confidence, each interpreter must nevertheless choose among the various options. I have chosen to locate the writing of the Gospel within the bounds of Israel, before the destruction of Jerusalem. The basic needs that the narrator was addressing were the needs of Christians resulting from their mission to very real adversaries in the synagogue and temple. The giants whom they challenged were not dead but very much alive; they were the same giants that Jesus had confronted.[16]

Part Two

MESSAGES FROM A
VICTORIOUS MARTYR

The loss of the cross were to me
another cross.[1]

A word of postlude and then a word of prelude. As postlude:
We have tried thus far to get our bearings on the kind of conversation the narrator was carrying on with his first readers. We
have broken away from the habit of reading the Gospel with
eyes focused on the career of Jesus during the period before
Golgotha. Instead, we consider that in this case the primary
history is the later conversation. So too we have broken away
from the habit of seeking theological or moral lessons for our
own day. Rather, in this case we consider that the primary theology may be found in the narrator's thinking as he related the
life of his own churches to the story of Jesus, as that story was
mediated through the risen Christ speaking through the gift of
the Spirit.

As prelude: We now take up a different task. Basing our
study on specific texts, we will try to reconstruct various messages from the victorious Lord, messages designed to meet the
urgent needs of John's readers, sometimes of lay people and
sometimes of charismatic leaders. The literary form of a Gospel
requires that these messages be expressed by Jesus before his
death. However, that same literary form makes it clear that those
messages anticipated the situations of believers and disciples

after Jesus' death. Explicit provision is made for the later work of the Holy Spirit in reminding John's readers of "all that I have said to you." Accordingly, as those readers responded to each message, they would listen to it as a message coming to them from their living Lord. In John's writing and in their reading "a sharp distinction between pre- and post-Easter sayings of Jesus was not made."[2] So now we turn to a consideration of selected messages that convey the very substance of Johannine history and theology.

Chapter VI

MY PEACE I GIVE TO YOU

> Do you know, since the establishment
> of Christianity as a state religion,
> a single example of a state which
> really followed a Christian policy?
> You can't point out one.[1]

Not least among the messages of the victorious martyr is the pledge of peace. The words are familiar, for they have been cherished by countless generations since they were first spoken. Rarely, however, do Christians pause to study the full force of this pledge in its original literary and historical context.[2]

In the Gospel the pledge occurs three times, each in a highly strategic place. Twice it appears in the Farewell Address as the strongly emphasized conclusion of two segments (14:27f.; 16:33f.). In both cases it represents a gift that anticipated later needs on the part of the disciples. The third time it appears during Jesus' rendezvous with his disciples after his death, when the gift of peace marks his continuing presence with them (20:19–23).

The first context establishes clear boundaries of meaning. The peace is not a vague state of bliss in general, but *his* peace, something belonging to him that he alone can give as a farewell bequest. Nor is it spread on the winds for universal appreciation; it is given only to *his own*, those who belong to him and who are being commissioned to carry on his work. It forever links their work to his, their story to his.

Peace I leave with you;
my peace I give to you;
not as the world gives
do I give you.
Let not your hearts be troubled,
neither let them be afraid [14:27].

Even a superficial analysis of the text adds two other clues to the nature of Jesus' gift. The opposite of peace is defined in a double way. It is set over against the world's peace and against hearts controlled by fear. Both thoughts are essential.

How does the world bestow its peace? As we have seen, the narrator defines the world elsewhere as "the Jews" who will persecute these disciples as they have persecuted Christ. The story from the beginning, not to mention its climax in the Passion, clarifies what sort of peace the world offers: It is peace readily available to believers who keep their faith hidden, or who, like Judas, become informers, or who, like Peter, deny any knowledge of Jesus. The world bestows its peace on the compliant, the passive, the ambitious.

When the world's peace is defined the character of the fear is also defined. "Let not your hearts be troubled" means: "Don't be frightened by the authority and power of your adversaries. Don't be discouraged by the apparent futility of resisting them. Don't try to buy security by betraying me. Don't let your fear of death prompt compromises with my enemies. Only by fearlessness of the world's power can you discover the power of my gift." In other words, this message, uttered at the Supper, conveyed, in capsule, the whole thrust of the Passion story.

In the following verses the prospect is given in detail:

You heard me say to you, "I go away, and I will come to you." If you loved me, you would have rejoiced, because I go to the Father; for the Father is greater than I. And now I have told you before it takes place, so that when it does take place, you may believe [14:28–29].

What Jesus says here in prospect the disciples are to remember in retrospect. What he says about peace will derive its meaning from his going away (his death) and his coming again (his return to them forever). The peace that will overcome their fear of the

Jews is thus a sequel to the peace that Jesus exemplified in facing those same adversaries. Moreover, this text implies that such peace is not self-engendered but comes from the Father, whose greater power it embodies. Here we may detect a basic core of Johannine thinking: Jesus' fearlessness in facing death at the hands of the Jews (his peace) is the precise condition that gives meaning to his death and his coming-again; in both respects this courage represents the active power of the Father (not the God of the Jews; 16:2). Yet the truth conveyed by this power will be revealed to them only after the event has taken place and only when they verify the same gift of courage from the same Father. After his ascension they will meet behind closed doors out of fear, but he will greet them there with his peace (20:21). They will recall their panic at his arrest and the peace with the world that it bought; they will receive from the Father a peace that the world will be powerless to destroy. It is this peace that will give new meaning to the act of believing. Now to believe will be to rejoice at Jesus' going and coming, to love him in such a way as to share his courage, to continue his mission to the same world but without coveting the world's peace. We conclude that this gift of peace had a special resonance for his first missionary appointees.

But, as we have seen, the narrator wrote with his eyes on a still different group, the prophetic speakers for the Lord in his own churches after such disciples as Peter had been martyred. He wanted his own colleagues to listen to the same pledge and to prove themselves worthy of the same gift. Missionaries would continue to confront enemies who relied on violence to defeat them. Their dilemmas would qualify them for empathetic participation in those earlier scenes at the Supper, when Jesus had first given the pledge, as well as in the later scenes, when he had made the pledge good.[3] Further implications of that pledge may be drawn from verses immediately preceding:

These things I have spoken to you, while I am still with you. But the Counselor, the Holy Spirit, whom the Father will send in my name, he will teach you all things, and bring to your remembrance all that I have said to you. Peace I leave with you [14:25–27].

Again, we note a focusing of attention on the period after Jesus' departure yet an insistence on the importance, during that later period, of his earlier training. A chief function of the Holy Spirit will be to bind together those two periods. The text makes it clear that the two gifts are inseparable. Where the Spirit is, there is the peace also. Where this peace is, there its recipients are linked by the Spirit to Jesus' teaching before his death. This line of thinking had great significance for the charismatic leaders in John's churches.

It is probably true to say that from the first the gift of the Spirit to the churches has provoked turmoil and not least among the recipients themselves. An appearance of prophets has been the signal for the appearance of false prophets. That fact may not be obvious in Luke's idealized account of Pentecost, with its veritable explosion of charismata (Acts 2:1–36). But it was surely true of the church in Corinth, where the profusion of gifts created problems that tested the ingenuity of the apostle and may have caused a major failure for him (1 Corinthians 12—14). It was also true in the churches addressed in Mark 13:5ff., where Jesus warned against false prophets. So too in the Gospel of Matthew, whose edition of the Sermon on the Mount reached a climax in the warning against hungry wolves in sheep's clothing, who claimed to do mighty works in Jesus' name but refused to obey his commands (Matthew 7:15–27).[4] So it is clear that conflicts among charismatic leaders were endemic in the early church. We may even suggest that such conflicts helped to encourage the emergence of the Gospels as a literary genre, for if the commands and example of Jesus were to provide a standard by which to measure the authenticity of prophetic gifts, the churches would need trustworthy records of those words and deeds. It is such a need that we discern behind the editing of John 14.[5]

The student of John often finds that the narrator's deeper concerns are reflected in the repetition of the same teaching. In this case a specific promise, with the condition for its realization, recurs no fewer than four times within the space of fifteen verses.

> If you love me, you will obey my commandments, and I will pray the Father, and he will give you another Counselor, to be with you forever, even the Spirit of truth, whom the

world cannot receive, because it neither sees him nor knows him [14:15–17; also vv. 21, 23–24, 28].

What may be inferred from that conditional clause, "if you love me"? One safe inference is this: Leaders in John's churches were united in expressing their love for Jesus, as Peter did in chapter 21. Discipleship, in fact, was inseparable from such an affirmation. Yet it is significant that, in a Gospel where the theme of love is so prominent, disciples' love for Jesus is mentioned on only two occasions—here in chapter 14 and in chapter 21. And on those two occasions this love is neither commanded nor praised but rather is subjected to stringent testing. With this claim to love Jesus we should probably associate the following claims that are voiced in the First Epistle of John: We are in the light (2:10); we are born of God (3:9); we have passed from death into life (3:14); the Holy Spirit is active in us (3:24); we know and love God (4:7, 10, 20–21; 5:3). This is the sort of self-confidence that is the target of the conditional clause.

A second inference follows almost automatically. The text implies that the genuineness of such love must be doubted. Jesus viewed all these claims as problematic; especially in v. 28 he assumes that the condition has not been fulfilled. Just as the claims advanced in 1 John are fraudulent (3:18; 5:2f.),[6] so too the narrator in the Gospel aims at undermining the self-confidence of the charismatics, their confidence that they already love Jesus, who, in the time frame of the Gospel, is absent and invisible.

The text leaves no doubt as to the test of genuine love: "You will keep my commandments [14:15; cf. vv. 21, 23]" (in Peter's case the test is feeding the sheep). We may infer that to keep those commands is more difficult than to claim to love the Lord and that John's readers were content with the easier course. They were inclined to act as if the gift of the Spirit provided a degree of exemption from obedience to those commands. This is probably the reason why the narrator insists on making the gift of the Spirit wholly contingent on that obedience. He specifies an exact sequence: first, obedience; then, Jesus' prayer to the Father; then, the Father's gift; and then, the powerful works of the Spirit. In churches where many leaders were claiming to possess the Spirit, and where the communities had to distinguish true from false claimants, each step in that sequence is vital. And just as Jesus' peace is far different from the world's peace, so too the Spirit of truth is far different from the world's kind of spirit. The world that had rejected the commands of Jesus (in the sense of 15:18 and 16:11) was incapable of either seeing or recognizing the Spirit of truth. By implication, Christian prophets who did not first obey Jesus' commands were guilty of operating in collusion with that world and guilty of vast self-deception. They might have the spirit but not the Spirit of truth.

So the text invites us to conjecture as to the precise forms taken by that self-deception. One conjecture follows the clue of their claim to love Jesus. Their self-image as Jesus-lovers has encouraged them to confuse their ambitions as religious leaders with devotion to him. From their role as servants of the Messiah they get a sense of personal importance and security; the call to lead supplants the call to follow. They have not allowed the story of Jesus to redefine for them the meaning of such terms as leading, following, loving. Not yet has the revelation of God's love for the world changed the core-understanding of what love is. Rather, they have allowed unconverted conceptions of love to be the yardstick by which they measure their own devotion to Jesus.[7]

Another line of conjecture is prompted by the implication that they have ignored the necessary connections between possession of the Spirit and obedience to Jesus' commands. They do not doubt that they have received the gift; the emotional reverberations convince them of that. But such self-assurance is deceptive. There seems to be ample evidence elsewhere in the New Testament that the emotional excitement that often accompanied gifts of the Spirit induced indifference to the more rigorous demands of the mission to a hostile world. Such excitements could bring peace, but a form of peace that the world actually produces among rebels who try to escape from the anxieties and corruptions of life in the world. John may well have had this form of self-deception in mind when he used the demands of Jesus to puncture emotional afflatus and to encourage moral soberness. D. Bruce Woll has suggested another line of conjecture that has considerable merit. He pictures the narrator as mounting a strong warning against false prophets who arrogated to themselves the identity and authority of the ascended Messiah in such a way as to give priority to Jesus' exalted presence and to relegate to insignificance his earthly life. As a result, "the authority of the tradition of the prior work and words of the departed Son is threatened by appeal to the authority of the Spirit in the present."[8] Because of this threat the narrator stresses the obedience of the disciples to Jesus' commands as the test of their love and as a prerequisite for the gift of the Spirit. "The author subordinates the present word of the Spirit (and hence of the disciples) to the past word of Jesus."[9] We can easily understand that tendency on the part of charismatic leaders when we grasp what obedience to the "past word of Jesus" entailed. In chapter 14, obedience is defined clearly as taking the same road that Jesus had taken, the same *way* that Jesus *is* (v. 6). The misunderstandings of that *way* by Peter, Thomas, and Philip were the same misunderstandings that the narrator detected among leaders in his own churches (cf. below, pp. 103ff.). This insight on the part of the narrator leads him to close his chapter with the example of Jesus himself. In sharp contrast to the conditional clause addressed to his disciples, "If you love me [v. 15]," we find an unconditional manifesto: "That the world may know that I love the Father, *I do* as the Father has *commanded me.*" A parallel manifesto for the disciples might well read: "The world will know that you love me when you do as I have commanded you."

Two further things may be noted about the promise that the Father "will give you another Counselor [14:16]." First, the pronoun you is in the plural. John's concern was not alone with individual leaders but also with the entire leadership. This is only natural when we recall that each commune had a number of prophetic leaders. "The Paraclete is not the individualistic teacher within the heart of every Christian but a functional ministry within the Johannine community."[10] Second, the Spirit had a definite contribution to make to that group ministry in terms of specifying the commands to which obedience was essential: "He will teach you all things, and bring to your remembrance all that I have said to you [v. 26]." The gift of the Spirit was a matter not of emotional excitement, but of sober instruction, for how could disciples obey commands if they did not know what they were? Those commands were no vague generalizations or sentimental platitudes. We cannot doubt their rigor, even though the narrator does not specify in this text which commands he had in mind. To love one another (13:34)? To lay down their lives (13:38)? To do his works (14:12)? To ask anything in his name (14:14)? To bear fruit (15:4)? The form of the commands varied, but they were all issued in order to secure obedience; all helped to define the only way to the Father (14:6). None of them was easy to obey; thus each becomes, in its own way, a test of the claim to possess charismatic gifts. They were designed as controls to be respected by leaders who, left to themselves, would find alibis for disobedience by appealing to impressive spiritual powers. Self-deception was a nemesis for them, no less than for the Pharisees and high priests. The spirit of the world and the Spirit of truth are mutually exclusive, and the line between was drawn by Jesus' commands. There can be only one answer to the two questions, "Do you know the Spirit of truth?" and "Do you obey the commands of Jesus?"

Returning to the message of peace, we may now ask what new light this promise of the Spirit throws on the character of "my peace"? This context makes doubly certain the inference that the gift of peace, like the gift of the Spirit, is contingent on obedience to the commands of Jesus. Moreover, the coming of the Counselor will make such obedience possible by reminding disciples of the content of those commands. So peace and obedience are twins. So too are peace and joy. "If you loved me, you would have rejoiced [14:28]." Without the Spirit and its love for Jesus, disciples were unable to rejoice over the death of Jesus. We may surmise a corollary of the same logic: With the help of the Spirit they would be able to rejoice not only over the death of Jesus but also over their own death in line of duty. Such amazing joy would have the power to banish anxiety from their hearts and replace fear with faith. So obedience to the commands would mean the gift of the Spirit, would mean joy, would mean fearlessness in facing death, would mean peace.

Still other implications emerge when we consider the concluding verses: "I will no longer talk much with you, for the ruler of this world is coming. He has no power over me; but I do as the Father commanded me, so that the world may know that I love the Father. Rise, let us go hence [14:30–31]." Here the imagery becomes that of an all-out war between two rulers—Jesus versus the ruler of this world, that is, the devil. Every disciple must answer the question as to which ruler has the greater power. And John's answer is clear: The devil has lost his power over Jesus. Only a king who has proved his right to the throne can exercise such power. Jesus' gift of peace is a measure of his power as one who has defeated the devil. A similar idiom is found in the prophetic word of Jesus in Luke 10:18: "I saw Satan fall like lightning from heaven." Luke also linked to that same vision the power of the disciples over the same enemy.[11]

The contrast between two kinds of power becomes clear in the dialogue between Jesus and Pilate (18:33–38). The two rulers exercised two kinds of power. If Jesus' kingship had been of this world, his servants would have fought; in other words, his power over the world stemmed from his refusal to fight. The world's power, and hence its peace, depended on its readiness to use violence. One peace entailed fighting; the other renounced fighting.

These verses have the merit of restoring to the term peace its connection to its opposite, war—a connection that is essential in most popular thinking, in which peace marks the cessation of hostilities, the end of war. The same cannot be said, however, of Jesus' gift. His peace is made available in the midst of intense hatred and violent persecution, where it enables disciples to continue their struggle against the world. The war that this gift succeeds in ending is the war with the ruler of this world, when the devil loses his power over those who do "as the Father commanded [14:31]." That loss comes when, like Jesus, the disciples and their successors cease to be afraid of dying. Only in this sense does this peace mark the end of war. In this sense also the road to peace is the road to the cross. One might say that this message of peace from a victorious martyr is John's answer to the much later demand of Ivan Karamazov: "I want to see with my own eyes the hind lie down with the lion and the victim rise up and embrace his murderer. I want to be there when everyone suddenly understands what it has all been for."[12]

This segment of Jesus' farewell is concluded with the command: "Rise, let us go hence [14:31]." When we have fully assimilated the narrator's understanding of the gift of peace, we should be able to detect in this conclusion much more than its literal meaning. The minimal meaning is clear: Jesus summoned his disciples to rise and go with him across the Kidron valley to "a garden." Their obedience to this literal summons may be found in 18:1f. But in the Gospel elsewhere the movements of Jesus often have rich symbolic meanings, and we are not precluded from finding such values here.[13] This journey of Jesus symbolizes his voluntary acceptance of death as a mark of his love for the Father and his obedience to the Father's command. Thus this journey is an embodiment of his power over the ruler of this world and of the peace, courage, and joy that that power produced. He viewed the journey as a completion of his own assignment "that the world may know." Because this *going* was a going to the Father, it was a definition of his peace. This action spelled out the truth of two earlier statements in the same dialogue: "I am the way . . . no one comes to the Father, but by me [14:6]" (cf. below, chapter X).

But this final movement was not confined to the action of Jesus; it voiced a double command to the disciples: Rise, let *us* go. In the minimal literal sense they did obey him by going with him to the garden. But in a deeper sense they did not obey. First Peter, then Thomas, and then Philip had failed utterly to comprehend his parabolic references to this journey. They did not know where he was going or his strategy for getting there. In one sense they arose; in another they postponed that action until later. (The Greek verb to arise, *egeiro,* is the verb often used to refer to the resurrection.) They would not go with him until later, when, in recalling what had happened in the garden, they found the power and the courage to win their own victory over the ruler of this world. Then they would receive his gift of peace. Would John's readers, the charismatic leaders of his churches, be able to understand the full force of that double command? For them, the terms of that command would be transposed out of geographical movement into liturgical movement, as they read John 14 and pondered the decisions that that chapter identified with the gift of peace. From the beginning of the chapter to its end the narrator was saying, this is *his* peace and it is intended for *you.*

Chapter VII

WHEN YOU HAVE LIFTED UP
THE SON OF MAN . . .

Moses struck the rock twice, and first it gushed out
blood and then water.[1]

If he [Jesus] had not been pierced, so that there came
out of his side blood and water, we should all have
suffered from a thirst for the word of God.[2]

In telling the story of Jesus, John often takes pains to report
predictions that were to be fulfilled later in the story. When Jesus
makes a prediction and when that prediction is repeated, we
may be confident that the narrator considered it to be important. That is surely true of one prediction that appears three
times, albeit in slightly different forms. One version is this:
"When you have lifted up the Son of man, then you will know
that I am he, and that I do nothing on my own authority but
speak thus as the Father taught me. [8:28]." The curious reader
must inquire as to when this prediction was fulfilled. One might
be content with observing a general fulfillment in the magnetic
power that the cross has exerted in succeeding generations, but
the prediction itself seems to anticipate a much more specific
time, place, and personnel. Curiously, the story of lifting up in
chapter 19 does not appear to correspond to the prediction. It
does not seem to indicate anyone who at that place and time
came to know "that I am he." Have we perhaps failed to grasp
the narrator's understanding of the actual scene of crucifixion?
Does the text hide the fulfillment of the prediction?

Since it was the day of Preparation, in order to prevent the bodies from remaining on the cross on the sabbath . . . , the Jews asked Pilate that their legs might be broken, and that they might be taken away. So the soldiers came and broke the legs of the first, and of the other who had been crucified with him; but when they came to Jesus and saw that he was already dead, they did not break his legs. But one of the soldiers pierced his side with a spear, and at once there came out blood and water. He who saw it has borne witness [19:31–35a].

Step by step the story moves forward in a noncommittal fashion. Arrangements are made for the disposal of the three corpses. One corpse is treated differently; his legs are not broken but his side is pierced. From the wound an anonymous person sees blood and water flowing. So terse a summary leaves little room for any dramatic climax or any miraculous transformation. Yet the comment of the storyteller suggests that there is a hidden meaning somewhere.

His testimony is true, and he knows that he tells the truth— that you also may believe. For these things took place that the scripture might be fulfilled, "Not a bone of him shall be broken." And again another scripture says, "They shall look on him whom they have pierced" [19:35b–37].

Clearly, these are comments by the narrator, addressed directly to his readers ("you"). He declares that two separate scriptures have been fulfilled in what the soldiers did and did not do. He underscores the importance of the blood and water, as well as of the testimony of the anonymous witness, which he views as the basis for the faith that he desires for his readers. At few other places in the Gospel does the narrator so openly intrude his own appeal for his readers to believe. We infer that there is something hidden in this story that the first as well as later readers might all too easily miss. What is it?

We need first to identify the person who saw what happened and who gave his testimony to it.[3] Most recent commentators identify him with the beloved disciple.[4] My own view is that he was the soldier who used the spear. I think that the Zechariah prophecy indicates this:

I will pour out . . . a spirit of compassion and supplication, so that; when they look on him whom they have pierced, they shall mourn for him, as one mourns for an only child, and weep bitterly over him, as one weeps over a first-born [12:10].

The prophecy indicates that it would be the very people who pierced him who would look on him, and that combination of piercing and looking was true only of the soldier. Both the sequence of thought and the syntax of the sentence support this identification.[5] This man was certainly in the best position to see the flow of blood and water and to verify it with his testimony. Such an identification increases the points of contact between Zechariah and John: the act of piercing; the act of looking; the victim as an only son, as a firstborn child; the mourning; the spirit of compassion and supplication.

Who was this soldier? Probably a Roman, obeying the orders of Pilate.[6] But the narrator makes it clear that both Pilate and the soldiers were acting in limp subservience to "the Jews" (19:31). Their action becomes an index of the power of those enemies. When the soldier thrust his spear into Jesus' side he was striking the final blow for the Pharisees and high priests against the King of Israel. With his spear the soldier verified the full success of their conspiracy. Yet it is at this very moment that the amazing flow of blood and water signaled the failure of that conspiracy. The soldier was in the right place at the right time to discern the fulfillment of both prophecies. His unique role in the drama gave authority to what he saw and said, so that belief in his testimony becomes a recognition of the moment when the loss of life became a source of life and humiliation became glorification. We may well notice that this triple sequence of vision-testimony-belief occurs in three other places in the Gospel, and in all three what is seen is a heavenly truth, hidden from some onlookers but revealed to others (1:34; 3:11, 32f.).

Once we recognize the soldier as the anonymous witness and once we separate verses 35b–37 as the voice of the editor, we are able to follow the story line directly from verse 35a to verse 38. This story line links the action of the soldier to the actions of two other witnesses to Jesus' death: Joseph and Nicodemus. The three make an interesting trio: one was a soldier who was obedient to both political and religious leaders; another, a disciple who hitherto had hidden his faith; the third, a ruler of the Jews. Jesus' death produced surprising changes in all three; they all moved from tacit or open association with Jesus' enemies to public identification with Jesus himself.

In the case of Joseph, John stresses his earlier fear of the Jews, a fear that made him kin to other disciples after Jesus' death (20:19, 26) and to many of John's readers. Perhaps his success in hiding his faith is indicated by Pilate's readiness to grant his request, for the governor probably supposed that he belonged to the Jews who had demanded crucifixion.[7] If so, Joseph's readiness to disclose his discipleship by this dangerous public action proved that he had overcome his earlier fears. Later legend gave the spear carrier a name—Longinus—and made him a friend and fellow believer with Joseph. One textual variant suggests that the soldier even helped Joseph take the body down from the cross ("they took").

At this point Nicodemus makes his third strategic appearance in the Gospel. Scene 1 had told of his coming to Jesus by night, impressed by Jesus' signs but unable to accept the necessity of his own rebirth. In Scene 2 he had voiced his hesitation, as a member of the supreme court, in condemning Jesus without giving him a hearing; he had, however, kept his silence after hard-line colleagues expressed their suspicion of his softness (7:50–52). Now Scene 3 tells of a daytime trip that threatened an open clash with those same colleagues. Coming to express sorrow for a dead man, he brought embalming materials of such cost and elegance as to signal the burial of a king.[8] A "ruler of the Jews" here carries out a truly regal interment for "the King of Israel." Under this reading the story tells of three amazing conversions. The death of Jesus had succeeded in breaking through the solid front of rejection. In his death he had proved more powerful than his enemies, a fact attested by three witnesses whose former lives lent credibility to their actions.

Having explored the significance of the identity of the soldier, we now turn to examine the significance of what he saw. According to the narrator, that significance stemmed from the scripture prophecies that the event fulfilled. One such prophecy is given quite explicitly: "Not a bone of him shall be broken."

73

Where is that prophecy to be located? A major possibility is in the rule concerning the sacrifice of the Passover lamb, as found in Exodus 12:46 and Numbers 9:12.* We must realize that John dated this whole incident on the very day on which, each year, the Passover lamb was sacrificed. We must also realize that the narrator had introduced his account of the ministry of Jesus with the declaration by a prophet: "Here is the lamb of God that takes away the sins of the world [1:29, 36]." Perhaps he wanted his readers to link the event of crucifixion to this prophecy that had introduced the lamb to the world. If so, readers were encouraged to see at Golgotha a climactic example of "the sins of the world," an example, as well, of how those sins had been removed by the blood of this lamb. If so, the episode in chapter 19 is as telling an epitome of the whole gospel as the words of the Baptist had been, one epitome at the beginning and the other at the end. Just as Nicodemus appears at the start of Jesus' confrontation with his adversaries and reappears at the end, so the sacrifice of the lamb (no broken bones) marks the fulfillment of the prophecies of both Zechariah and John; one prophecy marking the first enlistment of disciples and the other marking the end of their training. "When you have sacrificed the lamb of God, then you will know."

In referring to bones, however, the narrator may have wanted to call attention to the words of Psalm 34.[10] This prophecy would have released a different set of echoes in the ears of the readers. The psalm describes a fateful struggle between servants of God and their enemies, who hate them because of their faithfulness to God. The servants receive two contrary verdicts: They are condemned by their enemies, but the Lord intervenes to reverse that verdict (34:17, 21). By preserving the bones of "one poor man" God assures them all of deliverance but without diminishing their vulnerability to suffering.

---

*There are other details as well linking these two texts. For example, the rule that when the lamb was sacrificed a bunch of hyssop was to be dipped in the lamb's blood, and this blood sprinkled on the lintel and sides of the door to protect Israel's sons from "the destroyer" (Exodus 12:22; John 19:29).[9]

When the Golgotha story of the unbroken bones is screened through this scripture, it becomes a parable of how the death and deliverance of one man underwrites God's promise of death and deliverance for many of God's servants. So interpreted, it would issue a summons to patience, courage, and confidence to all latter-day servants. Is this what the narrator had in mind? If so, we can imagine how his readers, accustomed to the use of the psalm in worship, would react to the soldier's testimony.

Let us consider now the significance of the spear thrust and the flow of blood and water. This too is a fulfillment of scripture, and in this case there is little doubt of the text: Zechariah 12. But there remains much doubt concerning how John meant the flow of blood and water to be understood. One possibility is that he wished to show how the two sacraments of baptism and the eucharist had their origins in the event of Jesus' death; baptism in the water and the eucharist in the blood.[11] Another possibility is to suppose that the blood and water were intended to prove the full humanity and corporeality of Jesus, in order to refute the claims of a docetic Christology.[12] I am not content with either of these venerable hermeneutical traditions. I think the Gospel itself provides more convincing clues to the solution of the riddle, clues that are to be found in the predictions of Jesus himself.

Some of the predictions are general. This is true of the promise that his lifting up would be accompanied by a revelation to the very people who had done the lifting, or the announcement that the world would be judged when its ruler had been cast out. Jesus had spoken of the seed that would bear fruit only when it had fallen into the ground. In many ways he had assured his disciples that his death would become "the real life of men."[13] None of these promises is specific enough to explain the significance of the blood and water. But consider the following prophecy of Jesus, which would be fulfilled only when he was glorified:

> On the last day of the feast, the great day, Jesus stood up and proclaimed, "If anyone thirst, let him come to me and drink. Whoever believes in me, as the scripture has said, 'Out of his heart shall flow rivers of living water.'" Now this he said about the Spirit, which those who believed in him

were to receive; for as yet the Spirit had not yet been given, because Jesus was not yet glorified [7:32–36].*

Like the crucifixion, this prediction takes place at a festival and on the "great day" of that festival. Both scenes take place within the context of a Jewish misunderstanding of Jesus that induces them to condemn him (7:32–36). In both scenes Nicodemus appears as representative of the ruling council. In both, Jesus is viewed as the ultimate source of living water. The prophecy anticipates the time of glorification and the gift of the Spirit; the offer of water is limited to those who will then believe in him. Those who drink will themselves become fountains of living water, with fountains flowing from their bellies (*koilia* is euphemistically translated heart). The narrator probably had this prophecy in mind when he wrote of the water flowing from Jesus' side. For him, the spear thrust of the soldier, the maximum indignity inflicted by Jesus' enemies, marked the moment when the water began to flow.[15]

Do the earlier chapters furnish any similar clue to the significance of the blood? I think so, although here one must speak with less confidence. We have already noticed the Baptist's prediction of the lamb. Although blood is not mentioned in that prediction, every Jew would have thought of the blood of the lamb, sacrificed at the Passover, which had power to atone for the nation's sins. If John's allusion to the unbroken bones referred to that sacrifice, the allusion to blood would carry similar profound overtones. A still more specific prophecy in the earlier chapters should be considered: the discussion of God's gift of manna to Israel and its relation to Jesus' flesh and blood, given for the life of the world: "Unless you eat the flesh of the Son of man and drink his blood, you have no life in you; whoever eats my flesh and *drinks my blood* has eternal life, and I will raise him up at the last day [6:53–54]." Here the drinking of blood is made a condition for receiving eternal life; the blood is Jesus' blood, and to drink it is certain evidence that a believer "abides

---

*It is possible to translate this verse so that the rivers of water flow from the heart of Jesus rather than from the believer (RSV margin). Such a translation would make the thought correspond more closely to 19:35, but most translators prefer the translation I have used.[14]

in me, and I in him [6:56]." Did John here intend to refer to the eucharistic meal? Interpreters debate that question endlessly, seldom convincing one another. But without question there is a direct reference to the event on which the eucharist itself is based, a reference to the death of Jesus: "The bread that I shall give for the life of the world *is my flesh* [6:51]."[16] It would be in his dying that he would complete both his coming from the Father and his going to the Father. To drink his blood, therefore, is to receive life from him and to share in his vicarious dying.[17] Only with such an awesome implication can one explain why the saying was so offensive as to impel many disciples to fall away (cp. 16:1–3). Whoever drinks his blood becomes, like him, a seed falling into the ground. So interpreted, the two images are consistent: the drinking of water (chapter 7) and the drinking of blood (chapter 6). In both cases eternal life is made available through the continuing of Jesus' ministry after his death. Both predictions are fulfilled in the flow of blood and water from the side of the crucified, which the soldier had seen, to which he witnessed, and which readers are called on to believe. For the narrator, the testimony of the soldier looked forward to similar miracles that would accompany later martyrdoms.

Having said all this, we must also say that to point out connections like these between the soldier's vision and the earlier predictions of a fountain of water and the earlier commands to drink this blood is a matter of conjecture that is more or less probable but can never be certain. Not so the connection between the soldier's vision and the prophecy of Zechariah. Returning to that prophecy we discern these important connections:

- In both Zechariah and John there is an important conjunction between piercing and seeing.
- In both writings the piercing is accompanied by mourning, for the actions of Joseph and Nicodemus are actions that are typical of mourners.
- In both stories these mourners represent people who formerly belonged among the enemies, the rejection front.
- The one for whom they mourn is in both cases spoken of as a firstborn and only child.
- The *two* mourners in John's story may also represent "the

house of David and the inhabitants of Jerusalem [Zech. 12:10]."

- Their mourning may in both cases illustrate "a spirit of compassion and supplication" poured out by God in a most surprising way.

Now we may add one more significant feature in the prophecy of Zechariah: "On that day there shall be a fountain opened for the house of David and the inhabitants of Jerusalem to cleanse them from sin and uncleanness [Zech. 13:1]." "On that day"—it is the same day as the seeing, the piercing, the mourning. The vision of a fountain is important, for it is congruent with the rivers of living water (John 7), the spring of living water (John 4:7–15), and the flow of water from the side of Jesus. The function of the fountain in Zechariah is even more telling. It effects a cleansing from sin, of which, in biblical idiom, the blood of the sacrifice is a primary symbol. It also effects a cleansing from uncleanness, of which, in biblical idiom, water is a primary agent. The narrator of the crucifixion simply expanded on these two predictions. The blood of the slain Lamb takes away the sins of the world and the water flowing from Jesus' side bestows on believers the Spirit and life and enables them to become rivers of living water. I find, accordingly, in the brief verses in John 19, an awareness on the part of the narrator of the redemptive fulfillment of many prophecies: those of Zechariah, of John the Baptist, and of Jesus himself. And this fulfillment would have multiple implications for the faith and work of John's readers.

We may well ask whether Zechariah's prophecy formed a legitimate basis for the narrator's interpretation, or was that interpretation a wholly undisciplined flight of fancy? Here let me cite with approval the conclusion of Walther Eichrodt with regard to the message of Zechariah:

> It is the martyr's death of the good Shepherd (Zech. 13:7–9) and his restoration and glorification by God (12:8) which evokes the great penitential lament (12:10) from the nation which had rewarded him with ingratitude, and which therefore leads to a return to Yahweh, which forms the precondition for the absolution and pardon of the messianic age (13:1).[18]

Judging by those remarks, the contacts between Zechariah and John were more than verbal.

We know that Zechariah exerted a still greater influence on the narrator, for he uses another citation to celebrate Jesus' entry into Jerusalem, as these two texts demonstrate:

> Rejoice greatly, O daughter of Zion!
> Shout aloud, O daughter of Jerusalem!
> Lo, your king comes to you;
> triumphant and victorious is he,
> humble and riding on an ass,
> on a colt the foal of an ass.
>
> —Zechariah 9:9

> And Jesus found a young ass and sat upon it;
> as it is written,
> "Fear not, daughter of Zion;
> behold, your king is coming,
> sitting on an ass's colt!"
>
> —John 12:14–15

It is perhaps significant that John alters the wording of the prophecy. He deleted the words "triumphant and victorious," perhaps because the triumph could not precede the lifting up. He changed the command "Rejoice" to the more timely "Fear not," possibly because fear was the dominating mood until after Jesus' resurrection. The disciples were unable to rejoice until that event (14:28).

It is more important, however, to notice how this citation fits into the architectural structure of the Gospel, in which the story of the entry into Jerusalem corresponds to the exit. At the entry Jesus is hailed as King of Israel; at the exit he is condemned as the King of the Jews but is buried with royal splendor by one of the rulers. At the entry the daughters of Jerusalem are saluted with the words "Your king"; at the end Pilate uses the same words in satire against the Jews. The narrator warns readers that disciples will not comprehend the meaning of the entry until after the exit (12:16). Jesus' entry had aroused the fear of Jesus by the Pharisees; his exit overcame the disciples' fears of the Pharisees. Many of these contrasts are so subtle as to escape attention, and some of them may not have been intended by the storyteller. They are more likely to be detected when a reader moves directly from Jesus' appeal to the authorities in chapter 12 to the final exercise of their fear-inspired power in chapter 18. When one skips over the interlude of the Farewell Address, one moves from an account of the entry that was shaped by Zechariah 9 to an account of the exit that was shaped by Zechariah 12, with its pivotal prediction of the opening of a fountain of forgiveness and cleansing.

We may now sum up the findings as they have emerged from examining a wide range of prophetic predictions in chapters 1–12 and a brief story in chapter 19 in which those predictions were fulfilled. In all these chapters the narrator had Christian believers in mind and he wanted them better to comprehend the events on which their faith was grounded. In 19:35*b* he turned to them openly and confessed his reason for telling the story as he did: "that you also may believe." Belief in the soldier's testimony embraced two major components: confidence that the pollution of the world's sins had received cleansing in the blood and water, and confidence that among those who had lifted up the Son of man there were at least some who had been drawn to him by his love for them. Such belief would include a trust in the power of Jesus' love for his enemies as a weapon best designed to penetrate the defensive armor of self-righteousness and self-deception, along with other strategies of the devil.

Chapter VIII

ASK AND YOU WILL RECEIVE

Biblical narrative requires us to learn
new modes of attentiveness as readers.[1]

We will now explore a cluster of messages from the victorious
martyr that demand those "new modes of attentiveness" of
which the epigraph speaks. These messages center in the twin
motifs of asking and receiving. The importance that the narrator attaches to these motifs is shown by the frequency of repetition; within the space of three chapters they recur at least five
times. The reader will notice much variation in expression, but
among the variables certain features remain constant. Thus before analyzing the successive versions, we point out six of those
constants.[2]

• In all five versions it is Jesus who issues the commands
with authority, specifying the conditions and claiming the power
to fulfill the promises. Attentiveness to this feature requires a
lively perception of the origin and character of his authority for
revealing to the disciples the words and deeds of God.

• In all versions it is the *disciples* to whom Jesus issues both
his commands and his amazing pledges as a phase in the final
stage of their training. Accordingly, interpreters must keep in
mind the character of their assignment and the conditions
under which they will later pursue it.

• All versions are located *at the same place and time*—the supper table on the evening of Jesus' arrest—and yet all versions
anticipate later places and times after Jesus has gone to his

Father and the disciples have begun their work. Behind the various teachings, therefore, interpreters need to perceive the hidden axis between their hour and his (cf. above, pp. 26–28, 35–36).

• All versions point beyond the successive occasions for asking to the continuing intimate *relationships* between them and him—the relation of guests to Host, of friends to Friend, of branches to Vine, of sheep to Shepherd, of petitioners to Judge, of subjects to King, of prophets to Prophet. Accordingly, readers must remain constantly aware of this set of mysterious relationships that may be summed up in the image of mutual and reciprocal abiding.

• In all versions the narrator uses words and images not as self-contained concepts to convey historical facts or dogmatic truths, but as clues to *visible events* that in turn disclose invisible relationships, such as that of vine to branches. Accordingly, readers need to visualize the visible events that prompt both the invisible asking and the invisible receiving.

• Those events are described not so much by single, separate prosaic sentences as by clusters of *symbolic sentences,* each of which illumines and is illumined by the others. To understand this highly symbolic language, we should listen to entire paragraphs and respond to the entire tapestry of thought rather than to the isolated threads.[3]

Cluster One

Truly, truly, I say to you,[1] he who believes in me will also do the works that I do[2]; and greater works than these will he do, because I go to the Father.[3] Whatever you ask in my name, I will do it, that the Father may be glorified in the Son;[4] if you ask anything in my name, I will do it[5] [14:12–14].

In discussing this first cluster we will limit ourselves to reliable inferences from the text. To facilitate a checking of these inferences, numbers are inserted in the biblical text above to coincide with the five inferences.

1. The opening assertion, "Truly, truly," is a linguistic form that often signals the presence of a prophetic manifesto.[4] It im-

plicitly claims that what follows carries the authority of God, a divine revelation that Jesus as a prophet has been charged to pass on to these intern prophets.

2. A double condition is set for the activation of the divine promise: Those who ask must believe "in me," and such belief must take the form of doing the works "that I do." This condition obviously applies to charismatic leaders within the churches, whose belief becomes operative in works and whose works represent the activity of three actors: the believer, the Son, the Father.

3. The works of the disciples will be greater than the works of their master because of his death and ascension. Through them he will do greater works than he did before going to his Father. The journey has increased his authority to command and his power to fulfill their requests.

4. The works that they do—events in which their asking elicits his acting—will constitute, in ways comparable to his death, new events of glorification, in which the Son will continue to glorify the Father and the Father will continue to glorify the Son.

5. The entire paragraph shows the importance of the phrase "in my name." The asking is done in that name; in that name God provides what is requested. To use Christ's name is to appeal to his authority, and this enables him to act in, through, and under the obedience of the disciples. The pronoun you in this case is plural, signifying that the command and the promise are issued to the disciples not as individuals but to them as conducting a group ministry "in my name."

In sum, the paragraph presents a complex pattern of ideas regarding the work of the disciples after Jesus has returned to the Father. This pattern presupposes the pivotal importance of that "return" as vindicating his right to command and his power to fulfill his pledges. So too the pattern is oriented toward a single goal—not the gratification of individual desires but the glorification of the Father in the Son. What he has done in his journey (Christ as the Way is the basic theme of chapter 14) is what he will continue to do through them. The authority of his name will form the link between his own asking and theirs, between his own doing and theirs.

Cluster Two

I am the vine, you are the branches.[1] He who abides in me, and I in him, he it is that bears much fruit, for apart from me you can do nothing.[2] If you do not abide in me, you are cast forth as a branch and wither; and the branches are gathered, thrown into the fire and burned.[3] If you abide in me, and if my words abide in you,[4] ask whatever you will, and it shall be done for you. By this my Father is glorified, that you bear much fruit, and so prove to be my disciples[5] [15:5–8].

I have five comments to make on this text, comments that will again focus on the patterns of thought within which Jesus' command and promise belong.

1. Everything in this thought pattern presupposes the interdependence of the vine and its branches. But in this pattern there are three other essential components: the vinedresser; the nation Israel, of which the vine was a traditional symbol; and the fruit. As a consequence, one needs to keep in mind the whole symbolic complex: God, God's people, Christ, disciples, their converts. Again we note the concern for the entire community as a single whole, rather than for the work of individual "branches."

2. The whole image focuses on the contrast between two kinds of branches (disciples). Here the figure sets those who continue to abide in Jesus against those who do not. All are branches; some bear fruit and others do not. But this contrast in fruit bearing reflects the more ultimate contrast in the branches' dependence on the vine. Not to ask = not to receive = not to bear fruit.

3. Now the fate of those fruitless branches is depicted in traditional imagery. One set of branches (= disciples = charismatic leaders in John's churches) is pruned from the vine by God as the vinedresser. Those branches first wither ("you can do

nothing"), then they are gathered, and then they are thrown into the fire and burned. This is a direct appeal to biblical threats of God's final judgment, now applied to disciples who at first did abide in the vine but no longer do so.

4. In this statement appears the polar opposite of fiery judgment; here mutual abiding becomes the definition of salvation, in which all desires are fulfilled and the Father is glorified. The statement also makes two thoughts synonymous: Jesus abides in the branch when his words abide in the disciples.[5] This in effect excludes any notion of mystical ecstasy or Gnostic speculation; the authenticity of religious vocation is measured by faithfulness to the demands that Jesus has levied on these disciples.

5. Just as the whole paragraph separates one set of branches from another, so the conclusion accents the proof of true fidelity. Nothing is said about the sincerity of intention or the satisfaction of personal ambitions. Nothing is said about asking as a matter of presenting verbal petitions in prayer and of receiving gifts as miraculous answers to such prayers. The proof of successful asking consists of bearing fruit and glorifying the Father. Of such proof the supreme example is provided by Jesus himself (v. 9).

Cluster Three

You are my friends if you do what I command you.[1] No longer do I call you servants, for the servant does not know what his master is doing; but I have called you friends, for all that I have heard from my Father I have made known to you.[2] You did not choose me, but I chose you and appointed you that you should go and bear fruit and that your fruit should abide[3]; so that whatever you ask the Father in my name, he may give it to you. This I command you, to love one another[4] [15:14–17].

1. In this context the term friends implies much more than intimate acquaintance and mutual liking. In the Old Testament both terms, servants and friends, had been used of prophets as slaves and friends of God because they knew God's will and obeyed God's bidding (Exodus 33:11; Isaiah 41:8). In this text,

therefore, the narrator is continuing to distinguish two kinds of prophets within his own churches, comparable to his earlier distinction between fruitful and unfruitful branches.[6]

2. This statement seems to demand the perception of Jesus and his disciples as prophets, for a key to prophecy is a conferred knowledge of God through hearing the voice and grasping the will of God. The second key is also included here—the commission to reveal to God's people that knowledge and that will, so that God's commands can be obeyed. Jesus takes the role here of the master prophet, training other prophets to continue his work of revelation after his death.

3. Implicit in this emphatic statement is a rebuke against those charismatic leaders who are self-appointed; in a church where the gifts of the Spirit carry prestige and power, they have cultivated those gifts for their personal advantage. The narrator here paints a sharp contrast between these and the others whom Jesus chooses for this appointment. So too he limits his promise to those disciples who give priority to the bearing of fruit that abides. They and they alone have the right to ask in his name, with the assurance of an answer. Total dependence on him is thus linked to his guarantee of productivity.

4. John never tires of repeating the command to love one another. Why should this be so, unless he wanted to counter the inveterate desire to love oneself and to concentrate on requests for oneself? This message makes it clear that asking *is* loving and loving *is* asking. The measure of both is given without qualification: to lay down one's life for the other. And of that measure, the example of Jesus is equally unconditional. We cannot be far wrong to infer that this example embodies the wisdom that Jesus has received from his Father and has given to these fruit-bearers.

Cluster Four

Truly, truly, I say to you, you will weep and lament, but the world will rejoice; you will be sorrowful, but your sorrow will turn into joy.[1] When a woman is in travail she has sorrow, because her hour has come; but when she is delivered of the child, she no longer remembers the anguish [or per-

secution], for joy that a child is born into the world.² So you
have sorrow now, but I will see you again and your hearts
will rejoice, and no one will take your joy from you.³ In that
day you will ask nothing of me. Truly, truly, I say to you, if
you ask anything of the Father, he will give it to you in my
name. . . . Ask, and you will receive, that your joy may be
full⁴ [16:20–24].

1. The narrator is here describing a situation in the subsequent life of the disciples when this whole prophecy would be
fulfilled. Then the affliction of the disciples will be the occasion
for the hilarity of the world, yet their sorrow will turn into joy.
Two conceptions of that situation are possible: (a) their sorrow
over the crucifixion on Good Friday and their joy over Jesus'
return to them at Easter, or (b) their own deaths when their
enemies kill them out of a desire to serve God (16:2). I think that
the second possibility is the better choice (although neither option needs to be excluded) because at the beginning of this chapter Jesus had linked the coming of his hour to the coming of
theirs.

2. Here the narrator intended to compare the anguish of
the disciples (the plural you) to the travail of the woman (the
Greek noun *thlipsis* usually signifies violent persecution [16:33]).
The comparison focuses on the amazing transition between sorrow and joy, and this transition coincides with the act of giving
life to another. Again the visible event, when the transition takes
place, may be the hour of Jesus, but the stronger likelihood is
the hour of the disciples: their hour = her hour.

3. Here three things are seen to be simultaneous: the time
when Jesus will see them again, the time when they will rejoice,
and the time when that joy becomes immune to loss. In the
narrator's mind, when is that time? The rendezvous as described
in chapters 20 and 21? Or the later hour of their faithful testimony (16:33)? Martyrdom would make their joy immune to
such loss, as was the case in the story of Stephen's death, in the
book of Acts.

4. That day will be like his, that hour like his. It is when
they face the same emergency as Jesus faced in the upper room

that they may be said both *not to ask* and *to ask,* a riddle that John wants to emphasize. In what sense will they ask nothing of Jesus? In what sense will they ask something of the Father? The text itself offers few clues to the resolution of this paradox. A major clue we will examine later; here a minor clue is provided by the thing that God gives: joy. If, in sharing sorrow like that of the pregnant woman, they share her joy, they will not need to ask Jesus for that joy; they will already have received it through their participation in his life-giving power. But that same joy can be considered a gift from the Father, who alone can make such joy full and alone guarantee it from future loss.

Cluster Five

The hour is coming[1] when I shall no longer speak to you in figures of speech but tell you plainly of the Father. In that day you will ask in my name[2]; and I do not say to you that I shall pray the Father for you; for the Father himself loves you, because you have loved me and have believed that I came from the Father.[3] I came from the Father and have come into the world; again I am leaving the world and am going to the Father. . . . In the world you have tribulation; but be of good cheer, I have overcome the world[4] [16:25–28, 33].

1. This reference to their hour corresponds to a similar reference in 16:2. Throughout the chapter the narrator has in mind that crisis for which Jesus is preparing his delegates. Then, when their own loyalty will be on the line, his speech will cease to be a matter of figures and symbols and will become a plain and direct speech about the Father. When they give their own testimony they will learn the truth of his message about God. That hour of suffering/asking will be an hour of learning.

2. Here Jesus gives a most surprising definition of the asking: Their readiness to accept martyrdom will become in itself the form taken by the request. The action will constitute the asking. By its very nature this action will be a request made in Jesus' name, as their confession of his power and his life-giving love. Such a testimony a false prophet will be unwilling to make. The whole notion of verbal petitions has been replaced by the offer of self as a son of God.

88

3. At the beginning of the chapter it is said of the persecutors that they had not recognized the presence of the Father in the suffering of the Son. The ending of the chapter presents such a recognition. By their acceptance of persecution the disciples declare to their persecutors their knowledge of both the Father and the Son. "You . . . have believed that I came from the Father." Just as their self-sacrifice will constitute their asking "in my name," so too the fulfillment of that asking will come in the form of a divine revelation to the enemies, the disclosure that "I came from the Father."

4. The conclusion of this segment of the Farewell Address summarizes the narrator's view of the command and the promise. The command to ask is embodied in their tribulation in the world; the promise to give is identified with the joy of those who are given a share in the victory over the world. The world's rejoicing over their helplessness and humiliation will be overcome by the Father's love for the world, as expressed through his sending of the Son and the Son's sending of these representatives. There is a negative implication: Any prophet who refuses to ask in this way will not receive this gift of joy. Good cheer is promised only to those who know how the world was overcome.

Let us now summarize the thought patterns within which these five versions of this command-promise appear. In the first place, we have noticed multiple filiations of the command to ask. The act of obeying this command is associated with believing, with doing the same or greater works than Jesus, with glorifying the Father, with carrying out a group appointment and ministry in the name of Jesus, with total dependence on him, with bearing fruit, with knowing God and conveying that knowledge, with loving one another, with sharing in tribulation and persecution, and with witnessing by way of martyrdom.[7] In the second place, there are similar filiations for the fulfillment of the promise: the gift of God's glory, the continuation of Jesus' works, life in the vine, the productivity of the vine, the vindication of loyalty, the authentication of prophetic knowledge of God, the fullness of joy, participation in the love of the Father and the Son, victory over the world.[8] In the third place, throughout the discourse there is implied a judgment on disciples who do not *ask* in the way indicated and therefore do not *receive* what Jesus promised. They may claim to believe, but they do not do the same works; they may have been branches in the vine, but they do not bear fruit and thus they are burned; they appear in the churches as servants of Christ, but they are not friends who can reveal what Jesus has made known about the Father; in shunning the hour of trial they have forfeited the promised joy; to them Jesus is still speaking in obscure figures of speech; they do not yet grasp the strategy by which he had won his victory over the world.

One further clue should be followed if we are to grasp fully the force of this command to ask and this promise to give. This clue is provided by the narrator in his descriptions of Jesus' own asking. The whole Gospel presents Jesus as an exemplar for the disciples (e.g., 13:15). This is entirely true in the matter of asking, as shown in three specific texts. First is the statement of Martha addressed to Jesus: "I know that whatever you ask from God, God will give you [11:22]." This is exactly the assurance that Jesus later gave to his own. Even in this regard, the intention of God is for master and disciples to share the same privilege and power.

The second text presents Jesus at the point of making his own final and unconditional decision when his own hour had come. Is this grain of wheat now to fall into the ground and die (12:23–24)?

> "Now is my soul troubled. And what shall I say? 'Father, save me from this hour'? No, for this purpose I have come to this hour [an example of not asking]. Father, glorify your name" [an example of asking]. Then a voice came from heaven, "I have glorified it, and I will glorify it again" [12:27–28].

I believe there is a direct link between this episode and the later riddle (16:23–24), where Jesus seems to contradict himself by saying that his disciples will both ask nothing and yet ask for something. Jesus' prayer was answered immediately when he asked nothing for himself but only for God's own glorification. In that decision on the part of Jesus the ruler of the world was cast out and the judgment of the world had taken place. It was this decision on the part of Jesus that the narrator had in mind when he spoke of the disciples and of their asking and not asking. But the following verses make it clear that the disciples were not yet ready to understand or to obey (16:31–32). Not until after his victory had been secured on Golgotha would they become able to ask in such a way that their joy would be full (16:24). When they were enabled to share his courage, they would receive a share in his joy.

There is a third text in which Jesus' own asking provided a model for his disciples—the prayer of Jesus in chapter 17. Here the Farewell Address, including the five teachings on asking, reaches its climax. This intimate colloquy between the Son and his Father is timed, like that in chapter 12, to coincide with the arrival of the hour (17:1). In both texts it is significant that Jesus does not ask to be saved from that hour. Rather, his only concern is the glorification of God[9] through the fulfillment of his own assigned task. That concern prompts his prayer for the disciples during the period after his death (v. 9) and for those others who will be drawn into the flock through the word of those disciples (v. 20). Of course, the narrator reports the prayer in full confidence that the Father will do whatever the Son requests. Accordingly, this prayer is a mirror reflecting the narrator's understanding of what it means to ask and to receive. It is this understanding that he wishes to convey to his readers, and especially to those leaders who have received the Spirit and whose prophetic role included voicing the prayers of a Christian congregation.

Chapter IX

IF YOU ABIDE IN MY WORD . . .

A word is dead
When it is said,
Some say;
I say
It just begins to live
That day.[1]

In the Johannine community, where we have taken up temporary residence, all members understood themselves to be dependent on the gifts of the Spirit, although some were specially endowed with gifts that qualified them to serve as leaders, notably in worship. Primary among the latter were the prophets. In some texts the narrator kept their needs in mind, as, for instance, in the messages promising peace to the persecuted (chapter VI) along with the Messiah's instant readiness to answer their requests (chapter VIII). Other stories conveyed messages to the wider audience of believers, as, for instance, the report on Nicodemus' conversion and on Joseph's newfound courage (chapter VII). Now in this chapter we will look more closely at some teachings that were immediately relevant to both the prophets and to their listeners, because these teachings focus attention on the bond that linked them together—the word.

We have already seen that one way of identifying the larger group was to speak of them as those who believed in Jesus *through the word* of those prophets (17:20). The narrator wrote to them under the conviction that their only way to know the truth and to become free was to "abide in my word [8:31]." In addressing the smaller group the narrator used a somewhat different emphasis. Over and over again he reminded them that their love for Jesus and their claim to possess the Spirit of truth could be verified only by keeping Jesus' commandments (14:15–31; cf. above, pp. 62–66). Only in this way could their word be trusted as being in truth the word of Jesus and of his Father. In this respect, John's community may be compared with the church in Corinth, where, because of the plethora of spiritual gifts, Paul was impelled to place a premium on the gift of prophecy: "He who speaks in a tongue edifies himself, but he who prophesies edifies the church [1 Cor. 14:4]." We may suppose that in John's community there were many leaders who cultivated this gift of prophecy; some of them did not hold fast to Jesus' word, and there were others of whom it could be said, "my word abides" (15:7). Thus that word became an essential index. For believers, the most important link in the chain of command was the word of the charismatics; for the charismatics, in turn, the most important link was the word of the master prophet, Christ. Accordingly, it will be worthwhile to look closely at both these links in the chain of command.

In these three statements Jesus addressed three different groups:

You do not have his [God's] word abiding in you . . . [5:38]
If you abide in my word . . . [8:31]
If you abide in me, and my words abide in you . . . [15:7]

In all three statements the *word* is intended to serve as a link. In all three a noun word *(logos)* is joined to a verb abide *(menō)*. That is a strange idiom—to *abide* in a *word*. The verb is an important term in the Johannine vocabulary, with a wide range of potential meanings. In fact, *The New English Bible* uses nine words in translating it, including abide, dwell, continue, remain, stay, rest, find a home.[2] Yet none of those translations fits the noun word. How does a person or a community dwell or make its home in a word?

So too the image of a word dwelling in a person or a community is unusual. A word is something spoken, not something that takes up a permanent residence somewhere. In normal discourse, word is so innocuous that it sends no shivers of excitement. To focus attention on such a colorless term is bound to invite boredom. Despite that threat we must examine the term closely to recapture its strategic values for John. It may help us to be reminded by Northrop Frye that in the Bible, God's word is not so much an object as an activity, "a process accomplishing itself," nothing less than "God's speaking presence."[3]

To be sure, some of the meanings are trivial and casual. On occasion, *word* refers to vague rumors or to popular gossip (21:23), to a familiar proverb or a homely adage (4:37; 15:20), to a particular verse cited from scripture (12:38), or to the entire body of scripture (10:35; 15;25; 18:9). There is no need to look for hidden meanings behind such conventional uses as these.

On most occasions, however, more weighty implications are involved. I should immediately point out that in these texts the narrator did not always use the same term *logos;* that term did not wear a special halo for him. He could use the plural *(logoi)* to carry the same force as the singular (7:40). Instead of nouns, he often used various verbs for speaking. And he could substitute several nouns for logos without change in meaning, for example, voice, command, witness (5:25; 8:43; 12:50). His use of terms was flexible and we should try to match that flexibility in using synonyms and antonyms. Only by observing the diverse coordinates of the term word can we secure a firmer grasp of the patterns of his thinking. Keeping this objective in mind, we will examine several texts where significant reverberations may be detected.

First, we will study the prophetic utterance in chapter 5: "Truly, truly, I say to you,[1] whoever hears my word[2] and believes him who sent me,[3] has eternal life; he does not come into judgment, but has passed from death to life[4] [v. 24]." We will comment on the four phrases as numbered above.

1. The first few words mark what follows as the authoritative disclosure by a prophet who is speaking for the Most High. The prophet is revealing a reality that is normally hidden and he is vouching for its truth. The word is not his but God's. It should therefore be taken with the utmost seriousness.

2. There is a subtle difference, yet a close correlation, be-

tween hearing *me* and hearing *my word.* Jesus is not heard directly but only through his word. Yet where that word is heard, there Jesus is present. This distinction is highly relevant to both the narrator and his readers, because they had not seen Jesus himself before his death and because their only access to him now is by listening to his word as it is being mediated through someone else. This fact helps to explain why John placed such a heavy emphasis on hearing this word.

3. Here we detect a clear and concise definition of what it means to listen—to believe in God. And this is not merely a vague acceptance of God's existence but a specific conviction that God had sent Jesus. The act of sending was in the past, but "my word" makes that past act a present reality. Hearing, obeying, believing—these responses establish a bond between this Sender, this messenger, and these auditors.

4. Now the power of the word to transform the human prospect is revealed. That word spells freedom from the final judgment in that the auditor has already, through the act of believing, passed from death into life. Far more than a series of verbal sounds, far more than an expression of ideas and teachings, this word operates as a power to beget life. To speak this word is to speak of a vast mystery and an incredible miracle; to listen to it is to be offered God's own eternal life. The speech line is nothing less than a lifeline.

In the following verses the narrator declares that even the dead will hear the voice (= the word) of the Son of God and that those who hear that voice will live. So the word has the power to break through even the barriers erected by death and the tomb. The narrator also views the word as spanning the distance between present and future: "The hour is coming and now is." Because the Son carries within himself the Father's life, he carries authority to execute judgment—by his word alone (vv. 25–29).

In the preceding paragraph (vv. 19–24) John gives further clues to the origin of this word. It does not begin with the Son, who can do nothing by his own power and authority, but with God. In one sense it begins with a vision, with what the Son sees.

What he sees, in turn, is not an esoteric fantasy of a distant realm, but what the Father is doing in each earthly situation. It is because the Son sees his Father raising the dead and giving them life that his own word, his own speech to his hearers, is capable of raising the dead and giving them a place in which to live.

The narrator places the whole discussion in the context of a debate between Jesus and the Jews on the occasion of a festival in Jerusalem. The debate has been provoked by the sabbath-day cure of an incurable paralytic. The cure is spoken of as a word of Jesus in which he witnesses to the Father and the Father witnesses to Jesus. Yet it is that very word-witness-cure that induces murderous fury on the part of the Jews. They receive this blunt judgment: "The Father who sent me has himself borne witness to me. His voice you have never heard, his form you have never seen, and you do not have his word abiding in you, for you do not believe him whom he has sent [vv. 37–38]." We should observe an intentional parallel to verse 24. There, to believe in Jesus' word is to believe in the God who sent him; here, to believe in God's witness is to believe in Jesus, who has been sent by God. Here that word creates a harsh division between two communities, only one of which is faithful to the converging testimonies of Moses, the scriptures, the Baptist, Jesus, and even God, the ultimate standard of truth. More than this, the word exerts power to create its own habitat, a community that is characterized by prophetic audition (it has heard God's voice), by prophetic vision (it has seen God's form), and by continuing prophetic guidance (the word abides among them).

It is well to ask where these testimonies are being given. The narrator seems to visualize a dual courtroom scene, earthly and heavenly.[4] When the Jews accuse Jesus of defying the law, Jesus reverses the charges. In this conflict between charge and countercharge the reliability of supporting testimonies becomes decisive. The witness of Jesus is supported by his works and by a long chain of prophetic witnesses, who not only support him but also become the accusers of the Jews who, by refusing to come to him, demonstrate the truth of his charge: "You do not have the love of God within you [v. 42]." In this cosmic judgment scene the logos becomes not only the boundary between the two communities but also the grounds on which God renders a double verdict. The response to the word has become the action by which listeners draw on themselves the coming final judgment.

A somewhat different set of images clusters around the word in the debates of chapter 6, which form a decisive turning point in the story line. Here it becomes clear that the conflict between Jesus and his adversaries is inescapable, and that it has the result of producing deep divisions among the disciples. At the conclusion of the debates we note two sayings that reflect the narrator's special interest in those divisions. Looking back on the conflict, Jesus says to those disciples, "The words [*hremata*] which I have spoken to you are spirit and life [v. 63]." Peter's response confirms that assertion: "You have the words [*hremata*] of eternal life [v. 68]." In the earlier dialogue, however, Jesus speaks of other ways of entering into that life. Believing in the words is one way; another way is this: "Whoever eats my flesh and drinks my blood has eternal life [v. 54]." Believing the words and eating the flesh become virtually synonymous. And in this chapter the image of eating the flesh becomes the pivot of meaning. Jesus announces that this bread (flesh) is the only food for which people should labor, the manna that God had provided for Israel, the source of eternal life. As one image fades out, another takes its place: loaves-bread-manna-flesh-words. A key to the meaning of the whole series of images may be found in verse 51: "The bread which I shall give for the life of the world is my flesh." This assertion shows that, from the beginning of this episode, the narrator has had his eyes fixed on the Passion, when Jesus had given himself for the life of the world. That gift *is* the word of eternal life. The response to that gift is the critical choice facing both the Jews and the disciples: "Unless you eat the flesh of the Son of man and drink his blood, you have no life in you; whoever eats my flesh and drinks my blood has eternal life [vv. 53–54]."

In short, the words of eternal life constitute a demand from God to eat this flesh and drink this blood. In no text of the New Testament is the paradoxical conjunction of death and life more emphatic: "Whoever eats me will live because of me [v. 57]." The primary reference is not to the eucharist, but to the cross. If the eucharist is involved, it is only so by way of celebrating an actual sacrificial dying "for the life of the world."[5]

It is this reference to death that provokes rejection on the part of the Jews; they could not make sense of God's notion of giving "us his flesh to eat." It also induced a rejection on the part of the disciples, although they may have understood Jesus in part. "This is a hard saying [logos]; who can listen [akouein] to it [v. 60]?" The RSV translation is altogether too anemic to fit this context. Although *saying* is a possible rendering of *logos,* this context demands a wider, deeper range of connotation, because obeying this *logos* is a life-through-death matter. The preceding discussion has equated bread and drink with flesh and blood and then has equated flesh and blood with the giving of life for the sake of the world. That is why this *logos* is so *hard* (another weakening) as to cause disciples to take offense *(skandalidzein).* Here, no less than in 16:1, it is the danger of ostracism and death that causes disciples to fall away. Only when we understand the issue in these terms can we explain Jesus' reaction: "Jesus, knowing in himself that his disciples murmured at it, said to them, 'Do you take offense [skandalidzein] at this? Then what if you were to see the Son of man ascending where he was before? It is the Spirit that gives life [vv. 61–63].'" When this conversation is studied carefully it must be concluded that no passage in the Gospel makes clearer the totality of sacrifice demanded of the disciples or the subtle power of the devil's temptations (for Judas, 6:70; for Peter, 18:10, 17). To obey *(akouein)* this saying *(logos)* is to drink his blood, and that is to share his martyrdom. It is the awesomeness of that demand that alone explains the observation of Jesus: "No one can come to me unless it is granted to him by my Father [6:65]."*

In the close of the twelfth chapter, John summarized the final appeal made by Jesus to "the Jews" and their rebuff of that

---

*The function of this narrative in John 6 is, in some respects, comparable to that of the "Recognition Scene" in Mark 8:22—9:1. In both Gospels, readers are invited to discern the hidden connections between Jesus' role as Messiah and the necessity of suffering on the part of both the Messiah and his followers.

appeal. Accordingly, the words take on the thrust of a final manifesto that must be given later on by Jesus' disciples whenever their conflict with the world reaches an impasse.[6] I will italicize the various ways of speaking of the word.

I have come as light into the world, that whoever believes in me may not remain in darkness. If any one hears my *sayings* [*hremata*] and does not keep them, I do not judge him; for I did not come to judge the world but to save the world. Whoever rejects me and does not receive my *sayings* [*hremata*] has a judge; the *word* [*logos*] that I have spoken will be his judge on the last day. For I have not spoken on my own authority; the Father who sent me has himself given me *commandment* [*entolē*] what to *say* and what to *speak*. And I know that his *commandment* [*entolē*] is eternal life. What I *say*, therefore, I say as the Father has bidden me [vv. 46–50].

In this manifesto three correlations receive fresh emphasis. First, the word becomes identified with God's command; to keep this word is to obey what God commands. Like a true prophet, Jesus reveals only what his Father intends, and that intention is to communicate eternal life. Potentially, the command itself is a gift, the offer of life; to obey the command is to accept the gift. Note how the total mission of Jesus is comprehended within the various metaphors for speaking: the singular *word* or *command*, the plural *sayings* or the inclusive phrase *what I say*. When the narrator says *word* he is thinking of the story as a whole, of the word that Jesus *is*.

Second, we observe the close correlation between the word and light. Like the word and like eternal life, this light comes into the world of darkness as a command of God. One of its inevitable effects is to separate the two realms—darkness and light. Here the Johannine idiom echoes the Genesis story of creation. God speaks and gives an order; the order is obeyed; there is light. In the narrator's thought the word provides a direct link between every believer and the primal action of God in creation. Accordingly, when charismatic speakers of Christ relay this command, their listeners, by obeying, can move out of the primeval darkness into the light of Day One. The moment of obedience unites charismatic speakers and their Spirit-moved auditors with God's continuing creation.

Third, this same word, when spoken and obeyed, connects the community to the last day, when the same word that has come to save the world will serve as its final judge. It can hardly be otherwise if this word is, in truth, the word of the Father, who said, "Let there be light." Again we should become aware of the relevance of this idiom to John's readers. Whether in proclaiming the word or in hearing it, their action is placed within the widest conceivable horizons—the first day of creation and the final day of judgment. Yet those remote horizons come near whenever the logos brings them into contact with eternal life, that is, with the flesh of Jesus given for the life of the world.

It is as an epitome of these diverse nuances in the idiom of God's speaking and commanding that we should read the Gospel's Prologue.[7] When we turn from all the later logos references to the Prologue we will listen to it as a musical prelude that introduces many of the motifs which dominate the symphony as a whole. "In the beginning"—here the narrator traces the word, addressed to the churches of his day, back to the glory of God "before the foundation of the world" (cf. 17:24). "The logos was with God. The logos was God [1:1]." As Jesus constantly reminded disciples: "The logos is not mine but the Father's who sent me [14:24]." The sending of this Son by this Father belongs among the primal acts of creation. It is this God whom Jesus sees at work and whose word Jesus has heard, who sends Jesus and commands what he is to say and do. This authenticates him as a true prophet: His message to Israel is God speaking; his work among them is God at work. Their response to that word-work spells the difference between darkness and light, death and life. Where that word is, there God is. Those who believe that word join Jesus where he is, that is, with God. In the Prologue, as in the rest of the Gospel, the basic equation is established: word = life = light = glory. The Prologue declares Jesus to *be* that word; the Gospel later on declares him to *be* that life, that light, that glory.

I cannot myself attribute this Prologue to anyone other than the narrator. As a Spirit-guided prophet, he here screens the experience of charismatics and believers through the Genesis story of creation and at the same time screens that scripture through their communal experience of the glory of the indwelling Word (1:14). He traces the rebirth of all God's children to their belief in Jesus as God's message to them (1:12–13). He traces to the same source the grace and glory that have been received by the worshiping community. He gives his testimony to the single chain of command that constitutes a chain of being that reaches from the first day to the last. The word that every charismatic leader is commanded to speak and every believer is commanded to obey, is God's word by which God conveys eternal life through the Son. So we should read this Prologue not simply as a preface alone but also as an epilogue in which the stories of John's readers become fused with the story of Jesus and with the story of God's creative and redemptive work. As an epilogue, the narrator's summary carries the same awesome choice:

You do not have his word abiding in you . . .
If you abide in my word . . .

Let us now attempt to summarize the many ramifications of the Johannine symbolism of the logos, of "God's speaking presence" within the community of believers.

• The words of Jesus are seen to constitute the cohesive force that makes of this community a single family, all of whose members have been born by the same word of God. The same word that has brought the individual to rebirth abides within each congregation and within the whole family.
• The same force binds the existing community to all its ancestors and descendants; in each generation, charismatic leaders mediate the word and all who are born of the Spirit accept the word and live by it.
• The symbolism serves to bind the present community to the primordial origins of light and life "before the foundation of the world," so that all believers, by obeying the word, share in the creative activity of God.
• The same symbolism links the decisions being made in the present, whether by individuals or by groups, to the last day, to God's final judgment, and to the ultimate victory of life through death.

• Christ as the Word is a continuing reminder of the sacrifice by which he gave his flesh and blood for the life of the world. His presence conveys a command so *hard* that disciples fall away unless or until they see "the Son of man ascending where he was before [6:62]" and receive from him the gift of the Spirit.

• The idiom is both threatening and encouraging insofar as the same word induces disciples to accept violent rejection on the part of Christ's adversaries and to continue their mission to those adversaries with the same offensive message and the same signals of victory.

• The thought complex was indigenous to the prophetic and liturgical traditions of Israel. In their worship under the guidance of Christian prophets, Johannine congregations could sense their identity with the experience of Israel from the beginning. In using the psalms they understood that the same God continued to speak to them, and they continued to respond to him. So the word came to embrace their whole history.

How simple and how ordinary a symbol, yet how complex and how inclusive! As a stimulus to the imagination, it was able to fuse together aspects of human experience that normally tend to fly apart: hearing and doing, thinking and feeling, remembering and hoping, the liturgical and the ethical, the doctrinal and the mystical, the inaudible and the audible, the eternal and the historical.

Chapter X

NO ONE COMES TO THE FATHER, BUT BY ME

There's nothing like the Day of Judgment
for concentrating the mind.[1]

Interpretations of the title of this chapter have varied so widely
and have led to such disastrous conclusions that we must establish some kind of reliable controls if our own reading is to claim
fidelity to the author's intention. If we are to avoid fantastic
vagaries, a first step is to observe the literary context. What is the
unit of thought? Its minimum length is the three verses of Jesus'
dialogue with Thomas:

Thomas said to him, "Lord, we do not know
　where you are going. How can we know the way?"
Jesus said to him,
　　"I am the way, and the truth, and the life;
　　no one comes to the Father, but by me.
　　If you had known me, you would have known my
　　　Father also;
　　henceforth you know him, and have seen him." [14:5–7].

Those three verses are the minimum. However, to limit the conversation to so short a fragment is a highly dubious procedure.
Interpreters need at the very least to study the preceding four
verses in which Jesus made a prophetic announcement that provoked Thomas' question. And Thomas' question, in turn,
elicited another question from Philip that carries the thought

line forward. So the search for the unit of thought leads backward and forward until it embraces the entire discussion.

The beginning of this discussion should be placed at 13:31, where the narrator, knowing what he was planning to say later, introduces the motif of Jesus' journey: "where I am going."[2] The discussion of the journey does not end before 14:31, where Jesus summons his disciples, "Let us go hence." Between this beginning and this end the narrator is deeply concerned with the bearing of Jesus' journey (now drawing to a close) on the journey of the disciples (which will begin only after that close).

To clarify the connections between those two journeys the narrator has recourse to a typical literary technique, an interplay of questions and answers that discloses the misunderstandings on the part of the disciples and their correction by Jesus.[3] The four disciples appear successively as "point men." After a declaration by Jesus comes a question that reflects a misunderstanding of that declaration. This question gives Jesus an opportunity to clarify the disciple's confusion, but his answer provokes another disciple to reveal his own bewilderment. To observe this technique affords one kind of control.

As another kind of control, the interpreter must respect the original dramatis personae; in this case the only actors on the stage are Jesus, whose going holds the spotlight, and the disciples, whose going will take place later. Those disciples appear seriatim; their chief function is to voice difficulties in understanding the words of Jesus. Offstage are other actors to whom the narrator occasionally refers: unfavorably to "the Jews" (13:33), "the ruler of this world" (14:30), and Judas (13:26–30); favorably to the Father, to whom Jesus is going, and the Holy Spirit, who will come to guide the disciples (14:26). The disciples, we must remember, are not believers in general but those who are being trained to continue Jesus' mission.

Still another kind of control calls for distinguishing two time frames. One is the situation of the Passover, where the action is anchored, although, of course, the motif of the journey includes other times and places. The other situation, on which we have chosen to concentrate, is the conversation between the narrator and his readers as they face crises within the church after the deaths of the original cast. Although the narrator obviously wanted to tell about what had happened in the earlier setting, his primary concern is to disclose the bearing Jesus' journey would have on similar journeys at a later date. The story itself distinguishes these two periods (13:36, 38; 14:3, 7, 12, 16, 19, 23, 26, 29). These references to the later situation so dominate the conversation that readers can be confident that they constitute the major motivation for the entire literary construction. In this connection it is probable that the "I am" saying in 14:6, like similar sayings elsewhere in John, is "to be seen as prophetic utterance in which the risen Lord speaks through the prophet in the first person."[4] Moreover, the tense in the phrase "if you had known me" reflects a retrospective view of Jesus' ministry as a whole. In short, the storyteller has his eyes on the period after Jesus' death, although he can deal with that period only by assuming Jesus' foreknowledge of it.

The setting for this conversation is probably the persecution that is to be initiated by "the Jews," as described in 16:1–3. The narrator's central objective is to persuade the charismatic leaders not to compromise their mandate by "falling away." His technique is to use successive disciples as voices to anticipate the doubts and confusions of those leaders and to use Jesus' replies as ways of resolving the doubts and clarifying the confusions. Behind the immediate conflicts he wants them to perceive the power of the glorified Lord in his struggle with the ruler of this world.

One saying of Jesus at the outset contains three recurrent accents: "Where I am going you cannot follow me now; but you shall follow afterward [13:36]." The first accent falls on Jesus' own journey, "where I am going." This motif pervades the whole conversation from 13:31 to 14:31. All references to Jesus' going point ahead to a single event, which John calls variously the time, the day, the hour. His movement toward that event is mentioned no fewer than eleven times in thirty-six verses. Three kinds of movement are taking place simultaneously: Jesus is going to his death; Jesus is going to his Father; the ruler of the world is coming to exert his power. Of these movements two are invisible, but they are absolutely decisive, because they represent the collision between the two ultimate powers. It is important to notice that when the noun way is introduced, it is as a substitute for the whole clause "where I am going" (the Greek noun *hodos* appears only three times and then is dropped). The whole clause punctuates the conversation and implies as a sequel, "I am going to the Father."

The second accent falls on the blunt announcement: "You cannot follow me now." Although applied first to Peter, it applies as well, by implication, to Thomas, Philip, and Judas. Each of these disciples raises a question that unwittingly reveals why he is unable to follow now. In fact, they are all excluded for the same reasons as are the Jews (13:33). Because those questions reflect attitudes that were common among Christians in John's day, we will in a moment look at them more closely. Here I want to point out that one reason Jesus says, "no one," in 14:6, is to make it clear that none of them was as yet ready to go where he was going.

The third accent is more positive: "You shall follow afterward." This announces a linkage between his journey to the Father and their later journeys. It also presupposes a complete turnabout in the direction of their journeys, marking the difference between "you cannot" and "you shall." That change in direction would involve a reversal in knowledge as well as direction; "Now you do not understand . . . then you will understand." What is it, then, that stands between that *now* and that *will?* His death, which they must live through before they truly see him and know him, along with their action in following him, as the way to the Father.

Peter is the first to protest, and the protest is a blend of truth and error. Truth is expressed in his recognition that to follow is to lay down his life for Jesus. John's readers would credit Peter with good intentions. Where is the error? John leaves that for readers to decide. Is it his self-deception? Or a heroic self-image that a whiff of danger would destroy? Or the assumption that following Jesus called for using a sword to defend him (18:10–11, 36)? Or failure to link a love of Jesus to a love for his flock (21:15)? However Peter's error be explained, it prevented him from joining Jesus on his way to the Father.

Our chief objective here, however, is to study the reactions of Thomas. Thomas' protest was provoked by Jesus' statement,

"You know the way where I am going." (The plural pronoun you shows that Jesus is speaking here to all the disciples.) Thomas' reply combines a confession and a question: "Lord, we do not know where you are going. How can we know the way?" (In this reply the plural pronoun we shows that Thomas is speaking here for the others as well.) There is truth in what Thomas says: truth in the salutation "Lord" and honesty in the admission of ignorance. And there is also much common sense expressed in that expression of ignorance. Until a community knows its destination it cannot wisely choose a route. Where, then, is the error in Thomas' protest?

The form of his confession/question suggests where the error may be found. It lies in common human conceptions of journeys. It is typical of those conceptions to separate the goal from the route. In his initial statement Jesus used two terms: *the way* and *where I am going.* To Thomas, the *where* denoted the destination and the *way* denoted the path to be taken from here to there. In effect he was saying, because we do not know the goal we cannot know how to choose the best route. Therein lies the confusion that the narrator seeks to clarify. In clarification he attributes to Jesus three statements, all of which focus on Jesus' own journey as the clue to a true understanding.

The first statement is the familiar: "I am the way, and the truth, and the life." Among other things, this says that it is wrong to separate route from goal. It is wrong to allow the spatial, geographical image of walking to determine the meaning of the metaphor *way.* This way is a *person.* To go this way is a matter of choosing to "follow me." The route is no longer an impersonal road that covers the distance from here to there. Knowing the way is a matter of knowing "me." "If you do not know me, you cannot know the way where I am going."

If we visualize the debates among the prophets in John's churches, we may guess a reason for the accent on "the truth." One measure of true prophecy is the degree to which Jesus' journey to the cross is remembered as the only way for prophets to go to the Father. Do the prophets make it clear that eternal life is not a distant goal but the immediate personal action of following Jesus? Jesus *is* ("I am") what he does ("the way"); he shares his life with all those who follow him on his way to the Father. To know him is to follow him; to follow is to live. So much for Jesus' first effort to clarify Thomas' thinking.

The second statement is an exact corollary: "No one comes to the Father, but by me." In this statement three points call for comment.

1. *no one.* Because Jesus is speaking to his disciples, this in effect says, "None of you." The intent is to exclude disciples who fall away when they face social and religious ostracism or death (16:1–3). This negative corresponds to the positive "I am" of the previous statement; the truth of one statement stands or falls with the truth of the other.

2. *to the Father.* The word is carefully chosen: Father, not God. This is the same Father to whom Jesus goes in his Passion. If believers make a distinction between goal and route, the goal must be defined by the Father and the route "by me." Yet any such separation is almost immediately denied, for those who believe believe "that I am in the Father and the Father in me [14:11]."

3. *by me.* This clearly means that a disciple comes to the Father by choosing the same path. The image of Jesus *going* to the Father coalesces with the image of the disciple *coming* to the Father; one image is filtered through the other. Because it is true that "I and the Father are one," it is also true that "no one comes to the Father, except by me." In knowing and choosing this route one knows and chooses this goal—oneness with Father and Son. This is why the narrator can be so dogmatic, so apparently inflexible and intolerant, in stating the exclusion "no one." The second statement thus clarifies the implications of the first; in turn, the second is clarified by the third: "If you had known me, you would have known my Father also; henceforth you know him and have seen him [v. 7]."

Where the first two statements sound like dogmatic universals, theoretical generalizations irrespective of space and time, the third statement, by contrast, is a direct announcement made to a specific group of listeners at a specific time. The plural you includes all disciples as disciples. His death will make a difference in their knowledge of the Father. Heretofore they have not seen; hereafter they will see. By going to his Father, Jesus will give them a vision of that Father. This knowledge will enable them to become revealers of the same Father to others. Here we come in contact with the chief qualification of Christian prophets: such a vision of God the Father in the death of his Son that they are able to disclose dependable knowledge of that Father to unbelievers and believers alike. To see, to hear, to know, to testify to what they have seen—this is the chain of knowledge in which the prophets are links.

We earlier called attention to the choice of the word Father rather than the word God. The third statement impels us to look again at that distinction, for it is the road to the cross and the death on the cross that established the inseparability of Father and Son. Succeeding verses contain no fewer than eight variations on this theme:

To know Jesus is to know the Father (v. 7)
To see Jesus is to see the Father (v. 9)
For Jesus to be in the Father = the Father to be in Jesus (v. 10)
The words of Jesus = the Father's works (v. 10)
The authority of one = the authority of the other (v. 10)
To believe in me = to believe in the Father (v. 12)
When Jesus comes, the Father will come (v. 20)
When Jesus loves them, the Father will love them (v. 23)

These are all alternate ways of saying that the route and the goal are one, because the Father is present in the *way* that Jesus *is*.

But why did this distinction between *Father* and *God* loom so large in the narrator's mind? Why should a chapter that begins with a reference to belief in *God* (v. 1) immediately shift to a discussion of the rooms in the *Father's* house? In three chapters John uses Father more than forty times; by contrast, the term God appears only three times, twice to refer to the object of belief on the part of disciples and once to refer to the belief of their persecutors. Why this disproportion? The clue to an answer is provided by those strategic verses in 16:1–3. The enemies will murder the disciples, thinking they are offering service to God, and they will do this because they have not known either the Father or the Son. There is an illusion in their thinking of God that could be corrected only by knowledge of the presence of the Father in the coming and going of the Son.

John discerns the same illusion in the mind of Thomas because he, like the Jews, has not yet recognized the interdependence of Father and Son (14:7). That is why the disciples could not follow Jesus now, and why they would be able to follow afterward, when they had seen and known the Father in the Son's glorification on the cross (20:17, 28). Here, as elsewhere in the Gospel, the term Father "describes God as Jesus has revealed him."[5] Or, in the terms of Jesus' prayer, the hour of Jesus revealed the truth that the Father of Jesus is "the *only* true God [17:3]."

In at least fifteen other places in the Gospel the narrator makes a point of shifting from a reference to God (a term that often conceals religious illusion) to a reference to the Father, who becomes known as Father only through the work of his Son (1:18; 3:32–36; 4:21–24; 5:17–24, 42–47; 6:27–34, 43–46; 8:39–42, 54–55; 10:31–38; 11:40–42; 13:3; 14:1–2; 16:29–33; 17:1–5; 20:17). It is only through the Son's glorification that knowledge of God as Father has become possible. It is this Father-Son revelation that alone dispels human illusions about the presence and power of God.

It is the last of these shifts from God to Father that in some ways is the most illuminating. After his resurrection Jesus appeared to Mary and gave her this message for the disciples: "I am ascending to my Father and your Father, to my God and your God [20:17]." Thus he revealed to the disciples in a decisive fashion the "way where he was going" and he dramatically revealed as well their own identities as sons and brothers. Now the condition is fulfilled for his earlier promise, "You will follow afterward." Now his action interpreted his warning to Thomas: "No one comes to the *Father*, but by me."

We may now sum up the basic intentions of the narrator in shaping the dialogue between Jesus and Thomas. He clearly wanted to suggest the reasons why many disciples, like Thomas, misunderstood both the goal and the way of discipleship. He wanted to warn readers, in a blunt fashion, that the way taken by Jesus remained the only way to his Father. But he also wanted to relay a dependable promise: "I will come and take you to myself." Despite present confusions, they would be enabled to follow afterward, because they would then see and know things about the rooms in the Father's house that had earlier been hidden from them. It was the same readers who heard the warning "no one" who heard the words "don't be terrified [14:1]." The negative "no one comes" corresponds to another negative: "No one can come to me unless the Father . . . draws him [6:44; cf. v. 65]." This latter negative reminds us of various texts in which Jesus said of his own mission, "Of myself I can do nothing [5:19, 30]." And those texts correspond to the reminder "Apart from me you can do nothing [15:5]." It was because John's readers could grasp the truth of that negative that they could also welcome the assurance "We [the Father and the Son] will come to him and make our home with him [14:23]."

So the dominant mood of this chapter is one of movement; more than twenty-five verbs of movement are in the chapter—coming and going and taking. Each reader's imagination is invited to ponder the double or triple meanings of each of these verbs. With these multiple allusions to movement appear multiple metaphors of places: whence, where, whither. The discussion of the *way* ends with the invitation from Jesus to his disciples: "Rise. Let us go hence [14:31]." In our first study of this invitation we noted that it was linked closely to the promise of peace (cf. above, p. 68). It is linked just as closely to the understanding of the revelation to Thomas, "I am the way." In reviewing this invitation, C.K. Barrett mentions the three possible interpretations:

Rise from the supper table, let us leave the house.
Arise, let us go to the Father.
Arise, let us go to face the prince of this world.

Of these three, Barrett insists that the last two are "exegetically unacceptable."[6] I believe that this judgment ignores the thought patterns that pervade the whole chapter, patterns that center in the coming of the devil, the going of Jesus, the coming of the Father and Jesus, the misunderstandings voiced by the disciples (as surrogates for John's readers), and the anticipation of that later hour when they would see and know and go. In fact, I believe that for an exegete to limit the meaning to any one of the three, as defined by Barrett, is to repeat the confusions of Thomas and the other disciples. It is confusing to think of this *going* as the point of convergence of death and life, as the battlefield where the devil comes and the Messiah overcomes him, as an action in which God is revealed as Father of this Son, as the only path by which disciples can see and know this Father. Confusing, yes, but the narrator is claiming that this way "hence" is God's "truth" and God's "life" (14:6, 31).

It has become a commonplace of recent Johannine study to say that the only difference between church and synagogue was in their answers to the question, "Is Jesus the promised Messiah?" I find this tendency far off the mark. To John, theology was as controversial as Christology. Is God the Father of Jesus, with Jesus' Passion marking the only way to his house? And soteriology. Is salvation inseparable from following Jesus, as defined by this chapter? Or missiology? Does continuing the mission of Jesus to the world become the essential expression of seeing and knowing the Father? None of these -ologies can be separated from the others. In fact, John's choice of the image of going-and-coming preserves the integrity of thought more effectively than do these later, more technical categories.

This discussion of the *way* should help us understand the vast distance between John's perspective and that of the modern reader. John thinks of Jesus as a martyr whose martyrdom forced followers to accept that fate for themselves. He writes not for all future generations but for the leaders in his own churches. His eyes are fixed firmly on the situation after Jesus' death, although he can deal with that period only in terms of the Messiah's foreknowledge of it. As a messenger of the risen Lord, he combines the two time frames, pre-Easter and post-Easter. Such a perspective can only confuse modern readers, for whom the prospect of martyrdom has atrophied, and who naturally assume that the words "I am the way" were uttered before his death and that they establish for all time and all conceivable situations an exclusive doctrine of salvation, so intolerant as to seem bigoted in the highest degree. The greatest difficulty, however, continues to be the definition of "the way" as total self-sacrifice, rather than as total self-assurance offered to a religious elite.

Chapter XI

I AM THE RESURRECTION

A narrative miraculous in character is often
the best way to convey a mystery which may
itself not be miraculous.[1]

We have seen that it proved difficult for disciples to comprehend how Jesus could be the only way by which they could
come to his Father. More than this, the difficulty in comprehension was even less extreme than the difficulty in walking that
route. It was Jesus' example, even more than his teaching, that
collided head-on with their instinct for self-preservation. That
instinct, in turn, was a root cause of many confusions. It is not
surprising, therefore, that the narrator should want to dispel
some of those confusions. A similar cluster of confusions was
evoked by the magisterial announcement, "I am the resurrection
[11:25]." It proved far from easy for believers to grasp all that
was embraced by that declaration. To trace the narrator's efforts
to help them will be the objective in this chapter, and this calls
for careful analysis of the story of Lazarus.

I suggest three points by way of preparation:

1. I think it probable that John's readers, before becoming
Christians, had inherited, along with their neighbors, certain
notions that were prevalent, if not universally held, concerning
the nature of life, death, and life after death. Part of that in-
heritance was the tendency to think of those realities in
chronological sequence: Life is the period between birth and
death; death is the event that terminates living; life after that
event, whatever else it may be, requires some form of resuscita-
tion from the dead.

2. It is equally probable that in believing in Jesus as the Son of God, John's readers had come to believe, in a hazy fashion, that in dying he had won a vicarious victory over the powers of death. Because this belief contradicted their former notions of the basic meanings of these three terms, it produced pressures for them to modify their former notions, a procedure that is always difficult.

3. The collision between the older ideas and the newer ideas was so complex and so radical that the process of jettisoning the older ideas was at best halting and incomplete. We should expect that new understandings of life, death, and life after death, which would be more compatible with their faith in Jesus, would emerge only gradually, and only at the point where former misunderstandings were recognized and corrected by new readings of the story of Jesus. It is such a point that we encounter in the story of Lazarus.

In telling the story the narrator turns the spotlight successively on three groups: the disciples, the sisters, and the Jews. Each of these groups responds to Jesus' initiatives in its own characteristic way. The narrator deals with each group in isolation from the others, thus leaving their relation to one another undefined. So strong is his concern with these groups that Lazarus, whose demise provides the occasion for the conversations, does not speak in any of them. Only two brief verses are devoted to the miracle itself, and the question of whether or not it happened is not raised (11:43–44). The give-and-take of the discussions so dominates the story that one might readily infer that the happenings are shaped to illustrate the ideas at stake rather than those ideas emerging subsequent to the happenings.

It is the disciples who first occupy the center of the stage and who afterward become silent (11:7–16). So we must first ask what ideas were at stake in Jesus' interchange with them? At what points do they understand or misunderstand their instructor? Clearly, Jesus wanted to elicit their faith, and clearly, as well, this desire induced him to delay his trip to Bethany (v. 15).

One point at issue is whether Lazarus is asleep or dead. When Jesus says *asleep* they assume he means *not dead*, but when he says *dead* they assume he means *not asleep*. Sleep and death are terms with double meanings, and the narrator uses Lazarus to illustrate that ambiguity. There is a riddle here that echoes the earlier contradiction when Jesus announced that this sickness was not terminal, even though later Lazarus died. When is sickness mortal? When is a dead person asleep, and when dead? The disciples understand in part, but they are still confused over the relation of death to sleep.

A second point at issue arises in connection with Jesus' call to "go into Judea again [11:7]." They understand what that means, for Judea is the place where Jesus has just escaped a stoning (8:59). They were surely right in viewing Judea as an area of high risk. In fact, the raising of Lazarus would trigger the plot to eliminate not only Jesus (11:47f.) but also Lazarus (12:10f.). The disciples were also right in their willingness to accompany Jesus to Judea, although, in the light of Thomas' remarks in 14:5, readers might doubt the depth of their courage. How, then, does the narrator fault them?

We infer that their error is hidden in this saying of Jesus in 11:9–10:

> Are there not twelve hours in the day?
> a^1 If one walks in the day,
> b^1 he does not stumble,
> c^1 because he sees the light of this world.
> a^2 But if anyone walks in the night,
> b^2 he stumbles,
> c^2 because the light is not in him.

Many readers react to this declaration with surprise and befuddlement. It seems to be extraneous to the conversation, having no bearing on Thomas' question in verse 8, which finds an intelligible answer only in verse 11. Many interpreters have been persuaded by this apparent irrelevance to argue that the saying did not belong here originally. Yet we should be slow to relocate it, because John often intends to juxtapose unrelated sayings in order to prompt readers to search for relevance at a deeper level. That, I think, is the case here. The saying conveys an aura of mystery, because it shows that Jesus' thought was moving on a different wavelength from that of the disciples. The unexplained shift in the line of thought suggests that we ask at what point Jesus' attitude collided with theirs.

Before answering that question we need to examine the saying itself. It begins with the tritest of all truisms: There are twelve hours in the day, from sunup to sundown. But then the thought shifts to the contrast between day and night (a^1, a^2) and between light and darkness (c^1, c^2). Immediately we are in the metaphorical realm, where a distinctive Christian vocabulary is being used. Within this realm the saying focuses on the choice between stumbling and not stumbling (b^1, b^2). Readers are confronted with the alternative of walking in the day or the night; this alternative coincides with seeing the light and not having that light within one. These alternatives are presented with maximum seriousness; nothing is more important than to choose to walk in the day.

We can now answer with some degree of assurance the question of how Jesus' saying collides with Thomas' question. Thomas' question implied that the disciples as a group viewed death as the greatest evil; Jesus' reply implies that, on the contrary, to stumble would be even greater. To walk in the day requires that the fear of stumbling be so strong as to replace the fear of death. To the narrator, what Jesus *did* in this situation defined what not stumbling meant. He saw the light of this world (we should recall the force of *world* in John's vocabulary) and the light of the world was in him. But the narrator could not as yet say the same thing about the disciples; they still faced the crises summarized in 15:18—16:3. Would they and their charismatic successors choose to walk in the day, or would their fear of death prove stronger than the fear of stumbling? The answer to that question would prove whether they had learned from Jesus to view death and life from within the perspective of the true day and the true night. When they had learned that lesson they would see the hidden connections between the death of Lazarus, the death of Jesus, and their own deaths. Until they learned that lesson they would be confused by the apparent irrelevance of Jesus' teaching and example.* But if, when they faced their

---

*George Orwell may have had this Johannine motif of light in mind when he adopted in *1984*, as a watchword for rebels against the system, the apparently irrelevant saying, "We shall meet in the place where there is no darkness." For Orwell, the warfare between Big Brother and the one who had become the "firstborn of many brothers" (in Orwell's world, "Emmanuel Goldstein") was a war between light and darkness. The idiom of 1 John is similar: "Whoever loves his brother abides in the light, and in him there is no cause for stumbling [2:10]."[2]

adversaries, they would see "the light of this world," and if that light would be "in them," they would verify their residence in "the day" by refusing to recant.

We turn now to examine the conversation between Jesus and the sisters of Lazarus. For John's readers the picture of the Bethany home would doubtless call to mind the small house-churches of their own time. The sisters joined in confessions of faith in Jesus as "the Christ, the Son of God [11:27]." Mary adopted the posture of adoration and worship. It is said that Jesus loved these members of the family and even spoke of Lazarus as friend, a term used in this Gospel for believers (15:14.). The story is filled with idioms that were indigenous to Christian congregations: belief, signs, sickness, sleep, death, life, glory, world, day, night. Both in form and in content the story bears the marks of circulation in oral form among the churches, long before it was included within the written Gospel. In that oral form believers would easily identify themselves with the sisters; they would hear Jesus' remarks to Martha as addressed to themselves with revelatory albeit elusive force.

Martha is the first person who, on hearing of Jesus' approach, came out to meet him. John's readers would detect in her coming and in her words the marks of faith. Her first words indicate this trust: Had Jesus come earlier, Lazarus' death would have been prevented. A second remark also reflects her confidence in Jesus: God will give him whatever he requests (cf. above, pp. 90–91). She even speaks of her confidence that he is the Messiah "who is coming into the world [11:27]." Surely John did not fault her for such faith. But knowing his penchant for spotting both truth and error in the stance of believers, we must ask where in this case the error is to be found. This calls for careful analysis of Jesus' words.

Jesus first assured Martha that Lazarus would rise again. She assumed that he was referring to the resurrection at the last day and on that assumption, agreed with him. But we can infer from Jesus' reply that he wanted to correct this misunderstanding. She was right, of course, to believe in resurrection, but she was mistaken in postponing the event until the last day. In her answer she was simply reflecting expectations from the days before she had met Jesus. Those expectations were common among Jews, for in fact, belief in resurrection at the last day was the majority opinion among Jesus' enemies, the Pharisees. She believed in Jesus, but such belief had not changed her notions and had not softened her grief over Lazarus' death. Because her thoughts about death and life had not been affected, neither had her thoughts about resurrection. It was those baseline conceptions that were challenged by this new prophetic revelation from the risen Christ. That revelation constituted nothing less than an earthquake shock.[3]

a^1 I am the resurrection
b^1 and the life;
a^2 whoever believes in me, though he die, yet shall
     he live,
b^2 and whoever lives and believes in me
     shall never die [11:25–26].

The long story of Lazarus is recounted in part to provide a setting for this manifesto, which is designed to embrace the meaning of Jesus' whole redemptive work. The saying has the balanced rhythmic form characteristic of prophetic utterance. This form facilitates memorization and application to diverse situations and seasons. It carries the mysterious aura of hidden truth and establishes a direct axis between transcendence and immediacy, between the work of God and the situation of believers, whatever that situation may be. Its meaning does not lie on the surface; the saying is something of a riddle to provoke fresh thinking about such ultimates as death, life, and resurrection. Just as the example of Jesus furnished a new perspective within which to think about the *way*, so the story of Lazarus quietly placed Martha under subtle pressures to alter her thinking about life and death in the light of this unthinkable "I am."

The words are conducive to many interpretations, on which no single line of thought can establish monopoly rights. The power of the utterance derives in part from the impossibility of substituting a single verbal equivalent. Yet I think the poetic parallelism provides clues to the central cluster of meanings. For example, a^2, by being parallel to a^1, is roughly synonymous with it. To say that Jesus is the *resurrection* is to say that all believers who die will live through him. And to say that Jesus *is* himself the resurrection is to say that all thinking about a general resurrection at the last day must be radically modified to make it consistent with his life. Thus the story of Lazarus is a story that becomes relevant to all deaths on the part of all believers. For John's readers, who recalled the resurrection of Jesus in retrospect, this declaration would carry the awesome authority of their living Lord.

Similarly, b^2 is parallel to b^1 and helps to interpret it. If b^1 is true, b^2 is equally true. In this parallelism there is an added point, relevant to the present relationship between lord and believer: "I am . . . the life" is followed by "whoever lives . . . in me." He is not simply life, but he is also their life. The life that is "in me" is not subject to termination by death. This truth may also be illustrated by Lazarus, for his death can be called a sleep and his sickness can be viewed as a sickness not unto death. And this truth is relevant as well to Martha, about whom the narrator appears to be more concerned than about Lazarus. It is her misunderstanding that Jesus seeks to correct; and the sign of that concern is Jesus' question, "Do you believe this?" If she believes, such belief should produce greater change in her attitude toward death than is thus far apparent. Of course it is possible to accept her answer as being fully satisfactory: "Yes, Lord; I believe that you are the Christ [11:27]." Rather, I think that the narrator intended to fault that answer. She is unable to say, "Lord, I believe that whoever lives and believes in you shall never die." And at this point it is helpful to recall the narrator's concern for his own readers. Like Martha, they were ready to join in confessing Jesus as the Messiah. Like her, they also did not fully believe that Jesus is himself the resurrection and the life. Therefore, they were unable to affirm the parallel truth about themselves, as asserted in a^2 and b^2. To use Pauline terms, they could not fully share in the confidence that "whether we live or whether we die, we are the Lord's [Rom. 14:8]" or that their life "is hid with Christ in God [Col. 3:3]"*

To refer again to the parallel construction of this prophetic

*We may apply to both Paul and John the observations of Northrop Frye: "Resurrection is . . . not renewal or rebirth or revival or restoration; all of these words mean a new cycle of time, and are in the last analysis the opposite of resurrection. . . . As long as we associate the eternal with endless time, and the infinite with endless space, we have done nothing to get beyond our ordinary categories of thought and perception."[4]

utterance, it is entirely obvious that the two statements—*a¹* and *b¹*—refer to one and the same person, Martha's Lord. It follows that *a²* and *b²* are parallel statements referring to a single group of persons—those who believe in Jesus as the Messiah. In his role as the resurrection *(a¹)*, the Son of God is the one through whom believers who die will rise again *(a²)*, not to face judgment at some future last day but to join Jesus where he is. In his role as the life *(b¹)*, Jesus enables believers who live in him to share a form of existence not subject to death, because they have been born of the will of God (1:13) to a life that knows no end. The same believers both die and do not die. Their belief in him as the resurrection and the life is true, but it falls short unless it includes the truth of their own resurrection and life. The act of freeing Lazarus from death is the disclosure of a double truth that Martha, despite her profound respect for the Messiah, could not as yet grasp. And just as Jesus was concerned about Martha's faith, so the narrator was concerned about the faith of his readers. He was writing in order that by believing they might obtain life "in his name [20:31]." But he knew that they would find this confidence no easier to come by than did Martha.

I have already suggested that the narrator gave the Jews an important role in the story of Lazarus and therefore also in the disclosures concerning the meanings of death and life. In fact, both the story and the disclosures reach a climax in their action and reaction. The Jews first emerge in the background, as soon as the disciples point to the dangers of returning to Judea. They come to the foreground more openly as neighbors who come to Bethany to console the two sisters; they thus show that grief over death forms a bond of mutual understanding between believers and unbelievers. Although the sisters try to keep their meetings with Jesus a secret, these Jewish neighbors foil their efforts and take the center of the stage when Jesus openly challenges the power of death.

The narrator describes their attitudes as an amalgam of truth and error. Truth, in that they express their affection for this Bethany family and in that they recognize Jesus' love for Lazarus, which the narrator had also stressed (11:3, 5, 11). Error, in that they had supposed that Jesus' tears represented love-induced grief rather than indignation. In fact, Jesus had delayed his coming as an expression of his love. Thus the story illustrates two ways of measuring love, as well as different estimates of the meaning of death. Readers also discern truth in the realization by the Jews that if Jesus had been present he could have kept Lazarus from dying (v. 37). But the Jews were incapable of comprehending why Jesus should have intentionally stayed away.

The contrast between the two perspectives is dramatically underscored by the words that Jesus addressed not to them, but to God: "Father, I thank you that you have heard me. I knew that you hear me always, but I have said this on account of the people standing by, in order that they may believe that you sent me [vv. 41–42]." Here again the abrupt literary transition calls attention to the clash in attitudes. The radical rapport between Jesus and his Father calls attention to the equally radical alienation between Jesus and "the people standing by." Jesus knows that every request is answered by his Father (cp. above, pp. 82–85). There is perfect unity between the Sender and the sent (in contrast to the convictions of the Jews in 16:3). In his presence at the grave Jesus provides the linkage between heaven and earth, the now and the always, this death and the God who gives life (5:21). The situation provides Jesus with the opportunity to disclose the glory of God (11:4); but such glory cannot as yet be seen by the participants in the story, whether the sisters or their neighbors. To be sure, the narrator presumes to have knowledge of this mysterious interchange between Jesus and his Father (perhaps through the Paraclete-Spirit, given to him as a prophet). Moreover, his readers are also presumed to have the ability to sense the glory hidden in the Lazarus story.

Jesus' prayer indicates the central purpose of the story as a whole: "that they [the Jews] may believe that you sent me [11:42; cp. 17:3]." And the narrator perceives in the double reaction of the Jews a partial fulfillment of that purpose. The actuality of a positive reaction should not be overlooked: "Many of the Jews . . . believed in him [11:45]." This result is important. The death of Lazarus had become instrumental in spreading the gospel. Despite all misunderstandings among the disciples, the sisters, and the bystanders, Jesus had been able to reveal "the light of this world [v. 9]" and to manifest "the glory of God [v. 4]." John's readers would have been encouraged by this unexpected success, especially when they learned that it was this same crowd of believing Jews who had returned to the stage a few days later to celebrate Jesus' entry into Jerusalem as "the King of Israel [12:13, 17]."

But the negative reaction of the Jews receives a stronger accent. Their report about the raising of Lazarus, given immediately to the Pharisees, leads to the summoning of the Council and to the conspiracy to kill Jesus. In several ways this concluding paragraph gives a climactic resolution to the issue of death and life. Life for Lazarus means death for Jesus. To Caiaphas, Jesus' death becomes an essential way to avoid disaster for the whole nation. To Jesus, that same death is an essential way to give life to the world (6:51). "It is expedient for you that one man should die [11:50]." There are two expediencies, not one; and those two expediencies give two totally different meanings to the death of this one man. To his enemies, his death terminates the threat to the nation. To the narrator, this death, by its glorification of God, verifies his role as "the resurrection and the life."[5] So the plot to kill Jesus becomes the authentic climax to the entire story of Lazarus. The same plot proves how right the disciples had been to dread the return to Judea—and how mistaken. The conspiracy illustrates both the stumbling and the not stumbling as signs of light and darkness (11:9–10). It illustrates the relevance and irrelevance of Martha's ideas about "the last day" and the inadequacy of her partial belief in Jesus as the Messiah. Finally, the double reaction of the Jews prepares John's readers for similar reactions to their own mission among their neighbors. The story confronts believers with disturbing reminders that truth and error are blended in their own efforts to penetrate the mystery of how Jesus, through his own dying, has radically transformed the meanings of life, death, and the resurrection. To them, Jesus' statement "I am the resurrection" and his question "Do you believe this?" continue to require a direct, personal response.[6]

Chapter XII

WHERE I AM,
THERE SHALL MY SERVANT BE

The essence of chastity is not suppression of lust,
but the total orientation of one's life toward a goal.[1]

In chapter XI, I noted an amazing correlation between the
works of the Father and the works of the Son. The life of one is
the life of the other. The two **are** one, a oneness reflected in the
two I-Am declarations: I am the way, I am the resurrection. In
this chapter I call attention to an equally amazing correlation
between the Son and his servants. They will continue his mission, will experience the same unbelief and rejection, will imitate
his action of footwashing, and will share his peace. It may be an
exaggeration to say that "the experience of the followers of Jesus
will be a carbon copy of the experience of Jesus,"[2] but if it is an
exaggeration it does call attention to a basic truth. One expression of this correlation is the message adopted as the theme of
this chapter: "Where . . . there . . ."

In that theme we are still dealing with a prophetic declaration; this "I-Am" is related to the others with which we have
dealt. In this case, however, the spatial image intrudes and becomes a controlling feature of the thought; his *where* will become
the servant's *there*. The oneness of place becomes an image for
the oneness of persons. The "goal," to adopt Bonhoeffer's term
(see this chapter's epigraph), becomes the place toward which
servants move, and that place becomes identical with the place
where Jesus *is*. We have already noticed how frequently the nar-

rator uses the language of movement metaphorically and how rich in symbolism is his imagery of place: whence, where, whither.[3] This suggests that as a leader of worship, the storyteller wanted to help a congregation perceive the significance of two places: where it is and where it is going. This is why it might be argued that John never uses the term where without fusing together an actual and a symbolic location. He was an expert in theological geography.

This theological geography may begin as early as the first meeting between Jesus and those who were to become his servants. Two disciples of John ask him, "Rabbi . . . , *where* are you staying [1:38]?" Here we cannot doubt that the simple, homespun literal meaning is primary, but we would probably be mistaken to exclude any other nuance. George B. Caird puts the matter neatly:

Superficially this is a question about his address in Bethany, and the following verse picks it up at this level. But John is never content with the surface meaning of anything. At a deeper level he intends us to hear this as a question about Jesus' permanent home.[4]

The mystery of places recurs when Jesus, in his first interchange with a ruler of the Jews, describes rebirth through the Spirit. The movement of that Spirit is unpredictable and uncontrollable: "The wind blows where it will, and you hear the sound of it, but you do not know whence it comes, or whither it goes; so it is with every one who is born of the Spirit [3:8]." In this familiar quotation there is a shift in thought that many readers miss. The sentence begins with the reference to the whence and whither of the Spirit, but it ends with the whence and whither of "every one who is born of the Spirit." Their life, their existence after rebirth, has the same whence and the same whither as the Spirit. John expected his readers to understand the significance of this shift, in that it described their personal origin and goal.

John also wanted his readers to understand, with the Samaritan woman, the meaning of worshiping "in Spirit and in truth." That meaning included the discovery that the place of worship had been changed; no longer was worship dependent on a particular holy place, whether Jerusalem or Gerizim. Religious men and women could no longer determine the question of where they ought to worship by reference to previous places, however holy.[5]

Misunderstandings of Jesus' movements were inevitable whenever his listeners confused what he meant with his *wheres*. An example of this are the Jewish reactions to his statement: "Where I am going you cannot come. . . . You will seek me but you will not find me [7:34, 36; cf. 8:21–22]." One reaction: Does he intend to go into the Dispersion? Another: Does he plan to kill himself? Both were, of course, far from the truth. He and his adversaries were standing in the same place, yet they were talking about totally different places. We may suppose that John assumes that his readers would comprehend what Jesus' listeners had failed to grasp.

As we have seen, ignorance of Jesus' *where* was also the case with his disciples. No more than the Jews could they follow where he was going. They both misunderstood his speech about the *way* and they refused to join him. And it was not only an ignorance of his *where* but also of their own. "Whoever walks in the darkness does not know where he is going [12:35]." Jesus' theological geography was as mystifying to them as to his adversaries; that is, until after he had finished his course.

According to the narrator, a major objective of Jesus had been the desire that "where I am you may be also [14:3; cf. 13:36]." That objective is the basis for his promise to all his servants: "If anyone serves me, he must follow me; and where I am, there shall my servant be also [12:26]." This desire becomes the substance of his prayer for them: "That they may be with me where I am [17:24]." My purpose in this chapter is to explore some of the nuances in this promise and this prayer.

Because I am dealing with an image that the disciples understood only after Jesus' death, I will begin with the narrator's account of that period. A case in point is Mary's bewilderment in finding the tomb empty.[6] Her reaction is described with some care: "They have taken the Lord out of the tomb, and we do not know *where* they have laid him [20:2]." This complaint appears three times—ample evidence of its importance to the narrator. Mary gives much the same complaint first to two disciples, then to the angels, and finally to the gardener. So the text calls for close analysis. To whom does Mary refer in saying "they"? The best guess is that the reference is to the Jews who crucified Jesus and who kept control of the corpse, as was the usual practice in such cases. And why does Mary say "we" when she was alone? Perhaps because to the narrator she was expressing the ignorance and confusion of believers. Mary's words give no inkling that either she or they would take the emptiness of the grave as evidence of resurrection. The words underscore the importance of learning the true answer to the question where.

Her discovery surprised her so much that she ran to Simon Peter and the beloved disciple, and they, in turn, ran back with her to look for evidence to support her report. When they entered the tomb, the presence of the linen cloths showed that this had indeed been Jesus' tomb and that his body was no longer there. So the beloved disciple saw and believed. But believed what? I think he believed Mary's report and in effect agreed with her, "We do not know where they have laid him."

This inference, however, collides with the usual interpretation, which finds the disciple at this point believing in the resurrection of Jesus. I therefore need to justify my own deviation from the consensus. I am convinced that only if the two disciples shared Mary's consternation does the following sentence make sense, "They did not yet know the scripture, that he must rise from the dead [20:9]." Without that knowledge (which was open, of course, to John's readers) the two disciples were as baffled as Mary. So too the next verse contradicts any notion that the disciples already believed in the resurrection, for it says that they "went back to their homes." Such a trip is not a sign of faith but of continued illusion, of a calling frustrated and an apostleship halted (as predicted in 16:32). Furthermore, when the narrator comes to describe the first appearance of the Lord to the disciples (20:19–23), he makes no mention of the fact that two of them had already come to believe in the resurrection. Rather, that belief is grounded in the message delivered by Mary and in Jesus' own initiative in coming "where they were." Until that moment the harsh warning of Jesus had remained operative: "You are unable to follow me now."

Certainly the two disciples at the tomb had done nothing to clarify Mary's confusion, because when angels confronted her and asked why she was weeping, her answer remained the same: "I do not know where . . ." Nor did those angels do anything to console her, for they disappeared from the stage as soon as they had elicited her complaint, a sure sign of the narrator's intent. Even Mary's dialogue with the gardener preserves the same accent: "If you have carried him away, tell me where . . ." She is still baffled, and nothing has happened since her arrival to reduce her anguish. Only an unexpected word from the gardener could bring recognition, could terminate her grief, could answer the stubbornly repeated query. As soon as Jesus revealed his presence, he almost directly answered the query where. That answer was a double one: "I have not yet ascended. . . . I am ascending to my Father and your Father [20:17]." The mystery of the *where* becomes the mystery of his ascension, and the *where* becomes identical with the Father's presence. This, then, was the message delivered to the disciples; its truth was confirmed by his visit with them.

So John's theological geography is based on that reality expressed by the arrow: "to my Father and your Father." But that reality is not a remote other world, because after Mary had delivered her message, the ascended Lord came and stood among them, where they were. Now the mystery of the empty tomb is replaced by a greater mystery of a Lord so free of restrictions that he could penetrate closed doors and overcome their fears of their enemies. Having ascended to their Father he could come to them at will, could bring his Father with him, could share his Spirit and his authority. Because he was present with them he could now fulfill his earlier promises to them.

Two of these promises had explicitly anticipated his ascension. In the debate over what it meant for others to eat his flesh and drink his blood, a debate that had caused many disciples to stumble, he had raised the question, "Then what if you were to see the Son of man ascending *where* he was before? [6:62]." The events recounted in chapter 20 enabled those disciples to answer that question. Then they learned that it is "the Spirit that gives life [6:63]," that his gift of bread was the gift of his flesh, and that those who ate that bread would not die (6:50-51). The complex metaphor of *where* was a function of his vocation: Sent by the Father, he descended from him and ascended to him, and now in the same Father's name he could send out his own emissaries (20:21). Now those emissaries could know where they were going.

A second promise was issued in Jesus' debate with the Jews, after he had testified that he was the light of the world and they had rejected his testimony (8:12–30). As a rejoinder, Jesus had said: "I know whence I have come and whither I am going, but you do not know whence I come or whither I am going [v. 14]." Among their reactions to that remark, they asked a highly loaded question, "Where is your Father [v. 19]?" Going, coming, sending, being sent, whence, whither—all these terms were somehow included in the question "Where is your Father?" The elusiveness of the answer accentuates their hostility; the clarification of the answer in his ascension coincided with his commission: "As the Father has sent me, so I send you [20:21]." That clarification would still be highly relevant to many of John's readers, for whom continuing persecution and martyrdom would seem to demonstrate the absence of their Lord.

Where, then, did Jesus go? Only a multiple answer can begin to do justice to the mystery. As one basic answer, he goes to the Father who had sent him; this *whither* reveals the *whence*. He goes to dwell in his Father's house with its many rooms. As another basic answer, he goes "to his own." The departure to the Father coincides with an arrival among his disciples. Ascension makes this double movement possible. By going simultaneously to his Father and to his own he eliminates the distance between the two *wheres,* for when he comes to dwell with his own, his Father comes with him. Then there is a third basic movement in the ascension. His going to the Father enables the Son to send the Paraclete and also to speak of the presence of the Paraclete as a continuation of his own presence. It is when Jesus comes into the hiding place of the disciples that he gives them his peace, his courage, his authority, his commission, and as a way of unifying all other gifts, he breathes on them the Holy Spirit. So whenever they use any of these gifts that use is a manifestation where they are of the presence of the Father, the Son, and the Spirit.

Now, then, we may begin to grasp the massive meanings imbedded in his promise and his prayer. One of the multiple forms of the promise is this: "I go to prepare a place for you. And when I go and prepare a place for you, I will come again and take you to myself, that where I am you may be also [14:2–3]." In this text the mystery of the where is linked to the mystery of the when—"when I go." That double mystery is not readily reducible to words or to places. It is much more a matter of the correlation of vocations. When is it that Jesus "will come again"? Presumably, it will occur simultaneously with the act of taking these disciples to himself. And when will that be? When is it that they will enter the rooms in his Father's house? Readers engaged in the vocation that he has given them would ponder several possible answers. Would this be when they had loved him as he had loved them? When they have fully kept his commands? When he has been glorified in them and they in him? When they can say of their assignment, "It is finished"? The promise is clear; the time of its fulfillment is left undefined.

A second version of the promise takes the indirect form of an analogy, where again the assurance is unqualified, although the time of fulfillment is not stated:

a   Truly, truly, I say to you,
b   unless a grain of wheat falls into the earth and dies, it
     remains alone;
c   but if it dies,
     it bears much fruit [12:24].

Line b and line c represent an antithetical parallelism, which outlines the two options. There are two conditional clauses: one picturing the seed that dies and the other, the seed that refuses to die. And there are two opposing consequences: remaining alone or bearing fruit. It is *with* its fruit that the dying seed establishes its presence and unity. The opposite of aloneness is not simply to be with other seeds; no, the opposite of aloneness is the harvest, in which the vocation of the seed is fulfilled. The succeeding verse carries the thought a step farther. The dying of the seed is compared to hating one's life in this world; the harvest is compared to the gift of eternal life. The apparent aloneness of the dying seed is transformed into its presence with the harvest; herein may be perceived a parable of eternal life. The narrator sees this truth as initially exemplified in the dying and harvest of Jesus as the seed, but he immediately generalizes it to include all Jesus' followers who hate their lives "in this world." For them, the escape from eternal aloneness is given to them by the dying seed. All this is spelled out explicitly in the promise, with which we began:

a   If anyone serves me, he must follow me;
b   and where I am, there shall my servant be also;
a'   if anyone serves me,
b'   the Father will honor him [12:26].

Lines a and b are an example of step parallelism, in which line b represents an advance of thought over line a. There are at least three successive steps in thought: to serve = to follow = to be with. But the saying also uses synonymous parallelism, in that line a' parallels line a with no change in meaning, and line b' parallels line b with no change in meaning. The Father's way to honor the servants is to unite them with their Master. As an extension of the parable of the seed, these verses establish a fivefold equation: for the seed to die = to hate one's life = to serve = to follow = to be with. Behind the structure of thought lies a structure of personal relations; both structures convey a message similar to the allegory of the Father's house with its many rooms, where Jesus goes to prepare a place for his followers (14:1–4). In all this the narrator is not so much devising a general theory about life after death as disclosing to his readers the character of the life that is open to them before their deaths, through their deaths, in their deaths, together with the character of the harvest that Jesus promised.

John treats this promise as coming from the Lord who has won his victory over death. It is anchored in that revelatory utterance, "Truly, truly, I say to you . . ." But John also treats the promise as exemplified and verified by Jesus throughout his pre-Easter mission. This combination of time frames may well be illustrated by that baffling conjunction of tenses in the saying "the hour is coming, and now is . . . [4:23; 5:25]." C.K. Barrett writes: "From a standpoint placed in the period of the ministry of Jesus, 'the hour is coming'; from John's own natural standpoint within the life of the church after the resurrection and Pentecost, 'the hour now is.'"[7]

The same thought pattern concerning space and time, the where and the when, is present in Jesus' prayer for all believers: "Father, I desire that they also . . . may be with me where I am [17:24]." I will devote chapter XIII to the analysis of that petition.

Chapter XIII

I HAVE GIVEN THEM THE GLORY

God's glory is a wondrous thing,
Most strange in all its ways.
And, of all things on earth, least like
What men agree to praise.[1]

John is a master architect in designing diverse kinds of images. As we have seen, the image of the *where* is a complex spatial image not of a single place but of personal movement from a whence to a whither. Superimposed on that image of movement is the numerical image of oneness. To be where the Father and the Son are is to become one with them. And superimposed on this numerical image is still another—that of regal splendor, of God's glory. Where God dwells, there God shares the glory with those who are one with God. The title of this chapter speaks of that gift of glory to believers. The text where this thought emerges most clearly is the concluding paragraph of Jesus' prayer (17:20–26), which is itself the concluding segment of Jesus' Farewell Address, immediately before his arrest. The key sentences are carefully constructed to balance one another:[2]

Sentence One (vv. 20–21)	*Sentence Two (vv. 22–23)*
a^1 I do not pray for these only, but also for those who believe in me through their word,	a^2 The glory you have given me I have given them,
b^1 that *(hina)* they may all be one;	b^2 that *(hina)* they may be one

c^1 even as *(kathos)* you Father are in me and I in you,
d^1 that *(hina)* they also may be in us,
e^1 so that *(hina)* the world may believe
f^1 that *(hoti)* you have sent me.

c^2 even as *(kathos)* we are one, I in them and you in me,
d^2 that *(hina)* they may become perfectly one,
e^2 so that *(hina)* the world may know
f^2 that *(hoti)* you have sent me and that you have loved them even as you have loved me.

A brief analysis of literary structure may be helpful.[3] Each sentence has a single independent clause *(a)* out of which the dependent clauses emerge *(b–f)*. In each case the major clause deals with an action of Jesus, his petition for believers *(a^1)*, or his gift of glory *(a^2)*. This makes the thought of each successive clause hinge on the character and purposes of Jesus' work as a whole. The purposes of that work are expressed in six purpose *(hina)* clauses *(b, d, e)*. Among these six, some variation in formulation appears, but the basic thrust remains the same. Four purpose clauses deal with the oneness of believers *(b, d)*. The measure of their unity is indicated in two comparative adverbial clauses *(kathos, c)*. In turn, the substance of the world's belief or knowledge is expressed in two objective *(hoti)* clauses *(f)*.

Our concern with these two sentences is threefold. First, we seek the narrator's conception of the oneness for which Jesus prayed.[4] Then, we inquire about the bearing of that oneness on the world's believing. Finally, we will ask how the prayer is related to God's glory *(a^2;* vv. 24f.).

We must respect the integrity of each sentence as a carefully constructed unit of thought. Some interpreters, in eagerness to undergird an ecumenical passion, detach clauses *b* and *d* from their original roles in the sentence. Others support evangelistic passion by focusing attention on clause *e*. Such fragmentation almost always produces an anachronistic distortion of the original intention. We must also respect the author's intention, by balancing the twin sentences, to link the thought in each clause to the thought in its twin clause. For example, the believing (of e^1) is linked to the knowing (of e^2), while the content of belief (in f^1) is enriched by the content of knowledge (in f^2). Because each clause, taken by itself, is capable of a wide range of meanings, the interpretation of each clause must be controlled by constant reference to the vocabulary and imagery of the entire Gospel, and especially the farewell of which this prayer is intended to form the climax.[5]

First, we ask about the narrator's concept of oneness, which obviously represents one of his major concerns. The petition is stated simply and directly in b^1 and b^2 and then is repeated in d^1 and d^2. These latter clauses suggest that perfect oneness is realized when the believers are "in us." The measure of oneness is further specified in clauses c^1 and c^2; here oneness becomes a matter of reciprocal mutuality, relationships defined by the use of the preposition *in:* the Father *in* the Son, the Son *in* the Father, the Son *in* believers, believers *in* the Father and the Son. It is that mutual reciprocity that defines both the kind and the degree of oneness. By implication, this definition excludes many alternative (and highly intriguing) conceptions of unity; thus readers must virtually jettison many earlier ideas about what oneness consists of. To recapture John's way of thinking we must ask why he uses the preposition *in* so frequently. Obviously, there must be many reasons. What does it mean for the Father to be in the Son, for example? Among other things, it means that two subjects become active in a single action. This becomes apparent in Jesus' saying: "I do as the Father has commanded me, so that the world may know that I love the Father [14:31]." To be *in* the Father is to act in full accordance with his commands. It becomes possible for the world to move from ignorance to knowledge by observing that the single action of Jesus expresses the will of two subjects, the Father and the Son.

We have already observed the measure of the world's ignorance: "Whoever kills you will think he is offering service to God. They will do this because they have not known the Father, nor me [16:2–3]." It is this violent hostility that characterizes the world in Jesus' prayer; we go astray if we substitute other notions, the world as the physical universe, or the human race, or pagan culture.[6] In this context the world consists of God-fearing and God-serving religious leaders whose rejection of Jesus and his messengers reveals their ignorance of the Father's presence *in* the Son. These texts in John articulate the conviction that

ignorance of either the Father or the Son carries with it ignorance of the other as well. Conversely, the knowledge of one is
inseparable from knowledge of the other. The two terms are
interdependent; the revelation of the Father in this Son has
disclosed a unique mutual reciprocity. Whoever has seen the Son
has seen the Father. That is the mark of oneness.

In other words, we are dealing here with a single master
image—that of Father-Son. This Father is the one who gave his
only Son; this Son is the one whom this Father has sent to his
people. The gift and the sending, the coming and the going, the
dying and the victory over the world, are motivated by a single
command and a single love for the world, the supreme expression of which is the death of the Son in his glorification of the
Father. And that death/glorification discloses simultaneously the
power of the world and of its ruler. Accordingly, the martyrdom
of the Son becomes the measure of his perfect oneness with the
Father and of the Father's perfect oneness with his Son, whereas
the world's rejection is the measure of its oneness with its own
ruler. The prayer anticipates the hour when the followers of
Jesus, by believing in the Father and the Son, will encounter
violent rejection by the world. That world is as invisible as its
ruler, as powerful and as vulnerable, as deceptive as the lies by
which it safeguards its own survival. In short, it is "a powerful
collective person . . . the greatest opponent of the Redeemer."[7]
Yet in their martyrdom by the world, believers will be motivated
by a love for the world that exemplifies the oneness of the Father
and the Son.

This, then, is the conception of oneness that meets the
criteria detailed in c^1 and c^2. Such a rigorous definition makes
this petition worthy to serve as a climax of the farewell and
worthy to serve also as an anticipation of the Passion events that
immediately follow. Those events will verify the meaning of this
oneness by celebrating the victory of Jesus over the ruler of this
world. And from the perspective of the later time frame, those
events define the oneness that, as a result of the prayer to the
Father, will unite the entire family.

We now ask about the bearing of this oneness on the work of
securing the world's believing. A first observation is this: The
prayer binds together Jesus' petition for those who already be-

lieve with his desire for the world to believe *(a¹, e¹)*. Moreover, the sentences that define oneness also define what it means to believe. Contemplating the whole story of Jesus in retrospect, as the prayer does, the act of believing is now seen to include a readiness to act on the following convictions, that:

- the Father who sent Jesus to die for the world is the only true God;
- the prophet who died on the cross, taking away the world's sins, is the beloved Son of that Father;
- whoever comes to know Jesus as God's Son, comes to know God as Father also;
- in going to his Father, Jesus has made his God their Father as well;
- his word (17:20), reaching believers through his messengers, activates a chain of reciprocal interaction in which the Father becomes present in the Son, the Son becomes present in the believers, believers become present in both the Father and the Son and become so united with one another that their oneness becomes the fulfillment of this entire prayer.[8]

That is the gist of what believers believe. That is the pattern of convictions on which they act. And that is what Jesus, in his prayer, wants the world to believe and to know. Jesus has produced a oneness among believers that motivates them to produce a comparable oneness with people whom they will draw out of the unbelieving world *(e¹, e²)*. The entire pattern of thinking rests on the expectation that believers will become one through carrying on a mission that will elicit the same rejection and the same faith. The whole prayer moves toward a climax in the *hina* and *hoti* clauses, "so that the world may believe that you have sent me" *(e¹)*.

What is the world to believe and to know? The answers are explicit and surprising. The world comes to believe not that I (Jesus) have sent them (the messengers) but that you (the Father) have sent me (the Son). The world is to believe in the Father's love in sending the Son whom the world has hated. The believers must summon the world to believe in what they themselves have believed; the message is not about themselves but about the Father and his Son. The second sentence, however, carries the thought a step further: "that the world may know that you have loved them even as you have loved me" *(e², f²)*. When the hostile world comes to believe in the Father, that belief will carry with it the belated recognition that the Father has loved his witnesses (as martyrs) as he loved the Son (as a martyr), so that the one love of God may be known to embrace the Son, his messengers, and the world.

There is a profound irony expressed in all this, an irony that may become more apparent if we use two modern electrical images: the images of an insulator and a conductor. George B. Caird has made good use of the first image in describing how biblical authors often used various terms to protect the transcendence of God. Many devices have no referent other than God, but they are used as "verbal insulators between the holiness of God and the world." Caird mentions such terms as angels, heaven, majesty, tabernacle, power, name, and glory.[9] We may ourselves add the antithetical image of the conductor. Those terms that had been used in earlier generations to insulate God's holiness are used in the Gospel of John to emphasize God's oneness with God's Son and with all who come to believe in God's Son. The same terms that served as insulators now serve as conductors: name, glory, spirit, peace, power, love. On the one hand, this linguistic reversal expresses a savage irony, in that the same realities now insulate the leaders of the synagogues and temple from the presence of the divine holiness. Such irony makes all the more amazing and awesome the degree to which Jesus' prayer discloses in the oneness of his family the presence of the power, the name, the word, the love, and the glory of the Most High God. The contrast would seem to be complete; yet it is no more radical than the actual realities separating murderers from the murdered, and no more startling than the earliest Johannine intimation of the truth: "He came to his own, but his own received him not. But to all who received him, who believed in his name, he gave power to become children of God [1:11–12]."

We may now discern why John saw the oneness among present believers as essential if residents of the world were to be persuaded to believe. How were the insulators to become conductors? How could hatred be replaced by love? Where hatred had been grounded in the illusion of worshiping God (16:2) only a miraculous reversal in the conception of God would suffice. If the only true God is the Father who sent Jesus as his Son to be murdered by the world, belief in that Father can be conveyed only by messengers whom the Father loves as he had loved his Son, and only through messengers who show their love in the same way. So interpreted, the petition of Jesus was for a stupendous miracle, in fact, for a continuous chain of miracles: that believers in his word (logos) might become one with his Father and with himself, so that the love for their enemies might convey to those enemies a knowledge of the Father's love for them and thus convey the conviction that this Father is the only true God (17:3). Such an interpretation respects the integrity of both sentences, clarifies the nature of believing, and recaptures the narrator's sense of the calling of all believers.

It should be obvious why the narrator should have made this petition the climax of Jesus' prayer. His readers were facing conditions that strongly tempted them to give up (16:1). Those conditions provided ample reasons for doubting whether the Father actually loved either their enemies or themselves. Ostracism from their neighbors and their highly revered religious leaders created an isolation that seemed to exclude the kind of oneness that the prayer had stressed. Where, indeed, was the glory that Jesus had given them? So we turn to our third concern: the links that connect the prayer to the gift of glory announced in a^2.

To introduce the consideration of this gift, it is well to look again at the two sentences (above, pp. 132–33) that we have thus far treated as twins. The sentences are sufficiently alike to be called twins, yet they are sufficiently distinct to show that they are not identical twins. The second sentence moves beyond synonymous parallelism and marks a strategic progression in thought. For example, c^2 adds to the thought of c^1 by extending the unity of the Father and the Son to the whole company of believers ("I in them"). Furthermore, the belief (in f^1) that God has sent Jesus merges (in f^2) into the knowledge that God's love for the later messengers will be of the same order as his love for Jesus. Finally, Jesus' petition for believers (in a^1) reaches an intended climax in his gift of glory to them. When we realize that

John's readers, like the first disciples, were all potential martyrs, we should agree with Frederick Faber that God's glory is "least like what men agree to praise."

The second sentence indicates that all believers, through believing, become recipients of that glory, a gift of which the ultimate source is the Father and the intermediate source is the Son. The gift is a mark of their love for believers. On being called out of the world, each believer receives the gift which is denied all those who have not known the Father and the Son. Because the sender is glorified by the one who is sent, he glorifies those whom he sends, so that the same love that bound the Father to the Son now binds the Son to his delegates (7:18; 13:1, 31; 17:10). This complex pattern of thought even helps to shape the literary structure: The prayer begins (17:5) in God's gift of glory to Jesus, continues in Jesus' gift of glory to believers who have never seen him (17:22), and reaches completeness in the consummation to which the prayer points: "Father, I desire that they also, whom you have given me, may be with me where I am, to see my glory which you have given me in your love for me before the foundation of the world [17:24]."

In this petition the three images are clearly superimposed: whereness, oneness, glory. And a fourth is added: the gift of love. Moreover, all four images are here anchored in primal reality, emanating from the time before time, from "before the foundation of the world." The eternal Father has given all believers *to* his Son so that those believers already share in this primal reality; that is what happens, according to a^2, when residents of the world come to believe in the Word that they have heard from Jesus' delegates.

The same petition, however, is also oriented toward the future realization of this oneness, the coming consummation when believers will "see my glory." The final reality will disclose to believers the primal reality. What are the implications of this petition for the present situation of believers? They do not yet see this glory, are not yet "where I am," do not yet fully share in the primal love with which God has loved the Son. Even so, their act of believing links them to that beginning before all other beginnings, that end beyond all other ends—the glory and the love of God. Implied in this conception of the goal is a significant recognition of how to perceive the boundary between the world and the community of believers. Participation in God's love and glory forms an invisible barrier: "The world has not known you, but I have known you, and these know that you have sent me [17:25]." Yet the very purpose of believing is that Jesus' people may penetrate that barrier: "so that the world may know" (e^2, f^2). And we have seen how such penetration requires the sharing of believers in the perfect love of the Father and the Son.

In a word, just as the entire Gospel can be viewed as the testimony of one martyr to other martyrs, so too the prayer can be heard as the prayer of one martyr for others.* "I made known to them your name, and I will make it known, so that the love with which you have loved me may be in them, and I in them [17:26]."

Nowhere does the narrator specify the "lessons" he has in mind for his readers in his editing of this prayer; we are therefore limited to drawing inferences from the basic accents in the prayer itself. Petitions in such prayers usually reflect a need on the part of the praying community. For example, a prayer for unity implies that such unity may not exist; a request for being "where I am" reflects a sense of distance or absence; asking for love springs from the awareness of deficient devotion; a concern that the world may know discloses an awareness that the world does not as yet know and that believers are finding their assignment to the world anything but easy or effective. Such inferences as these are obvious and, on the whole, convincing.

We have seen that many other segments of the Gospel support these inferences concerning the problems being faced by John's churches. For example, the warnings that immediately preceded the prayer detail many of those problems. Any complacent assurance that his followers already believe is directly denied by Jesus (16:31). They think they understand his speech;

---

*The close connections that John draws between the gift of glory and martyrdom are not surprising when we consider that "the expectation of martyrdom was a daily feature of the life of early Christians. It permeated their consciousness, set the standards for membership . . . and consolidated the solidarity of the community in the face of the threatening personal apocalypse of its members, and especially its leaders."[10]

he denies such an understanding. The hostility they encounter will induce a scattering, "every man to his own home [16:32]." When they face the threat of death they will forget that he has already overcome the enemies they are facing (16:33). It is probable that some of these leaders, on that occasion, will pray to be taken out of the world, that is, that they will be excused from continuing so difficult a mission to "the Jews" (17:15). (In the book of Acts we have independent evidence that failures in the mission to Israel persuaded some missionaries to turn to the gentiles [e.g., Acts 13:44, 49].) But the narrator is convinced that any progress toward greater oneness with Jesus will require that his emissaries remain "in the world," whatever the danger or cost.

In this respect the situation of all believers, as reflected in Jesus' final intercession (17:20–26), was not very different from that of their charismatic leaders (17:7–19). Although they prided themselves on believing, they were loathe to define that believing by testifying to the world, when such testifying involved a high level of risk. They were not eager to define faith by love for the world but were more inclined to take pride in God's love for themselves. So they were not yet one with the Father and his Son. It is such a deficiency that is reflected in the central petitions of Jesus. Basic to the prayer is the conviction that all believers are witnesses, and that all witnesses are obliged to love the world that threatens to destroy them. Seen in this light, only an insensitive reader can be oblivious to the strength of such temptations as the prayer seeks to overcome. It was anything but routine for them, as recipients of the Spirit, to testify to the adversaries in their own neighborhood. Yet that was their task. The gift of the Spirit, like the gift of glory, would "convince the world concerning sin and righteousness and judgment: concerning sin, because they do not believe in me; concerning righteousness, because I go to the Father, and you will see me no more; concerning judgment, because the ruler of this world is judged [16:8–11]."

I conclude this chapter by drawing a series of three inferences. The narrator speaks of this gift of glory as a part of Jesus' intercessory prayer for believers.

Inference one: Those believers would listen to that prayer during a period of communal worship, so that their worship in his presence would make the gift intelligible to them. In his prayer Jesus links a vision of his glory to the experience of being "with me where I am [17:24]," a reference to his ascended life.

Inference two: The gift of glory is nothing less than a gift of eternal life with him; accordingly, the act of communal worship would help believers enter into that vision and that life. The complex image of being with Jesus where he is (i.e., of sharing his ascended life) brings the prayer of Jesus into a kind of correspondence with the story of Lazarus, in chapter 11, and with the story of Mary, in chapter 20.

Inference three: The patterns of thought about eternal life, as illustrated in these three chapters, became patterns of actuality as John's churches met for worship in the name of Jesus, as the risen Lord "prepared a table before them in the presence of their enemies."

Chapter XIV

LOOK! THIS IS YOUR MOTHER!

Never does the interpreter get near to
what his text says unless he lives in
the aura of the meaning he is inquiring
after.[1]

One of the most dramatic, if also enigmatic, scenes in the Gospel of John is the scene at the cross, in which Jesus gives his parting message, first to his mother and then to "the disciple whom he loved." Here is the triangular conversation, in which the two messages are carefully balanced:

When Jesus saw his mother and the disciple whom he loved standing near, he said to his mother,
  "Woman, look! This is your son!"
Then he said to the disciple,
  "Look! This is your mother!"
So from that hour on, the disciple took her to his own [19:26–27, paraphrase].

The scene may be treated in any of several ways. It may be considered a simple, straightforward account of what happened at that moment, as a definition of the personal relationships of three individuals. As such, the story invites the reader to imagine all sorts of psychological details, the play of emotions on the part of each participant in response to this crisis. At this final meeting Jesus demonstrated his personal affection for them as well as his responsibility to arrange for their mutual care after his death. It is almost impossible not to project the biographical stories of the new mother and the new son beyond this moment and beyond the reach of these laconic announcements. Until now Jesus had been their only common bond; now they would have each other and could depend on each other. Although the narrator does not exclude this kind of expansion, it must be said that he does not encourage it.

The narrator was more concerned with other things than immediate personal reactions. In fact, he records only the words of Jesus, not the verbal responses of either the mother or the disciple. No genuine conversation emerges. The narrator is content with reporting Jesus' command to look and his stentorian declaration, identifying a new set of relationships. John was writing years later, after all these people had disappeared from the scene. The mother and the disciple had both come to symbolize continuing features in the life of the church. Almost all interpreters grant the presence of many symbolic ingredients in the story, even though it may remain impossible to define those ingredients with confidence. The following observations point toward the presence of such ingredients:

• The story is located at the cross, where virtually every detail in the story carries multiple overtones, partly owing to the advance predictions: "If I be lifted up . . . "

• The reference to time, "from that very hour on," is significant, as dating the disciple's obedience to the implicit demand. His action derives special meaning from its relation to "the hour" of Jesus' glorification.

• Immediately following this conversation come the words "It is finished." It may be inferred that without this episode Jesus' work would have been incomplete. This gives a sense of high importance to the preceding scene.

• The call to look *(ide)* is a command often used by a prophet to accompany an authoritative disclosure of God's will. Human words become the medium for a message from God, announcing something unexpected, of first importance, and requiring instant response.

• The same command appears elsewhere in the chapter, and it is doubtful if the repetition is accidental. Pilate used the same command to announce Jesus as "a man" and as a king (19:4–5, 14, 19–22). All identities are important, yet all are hidden and all call for revelation: the king, the mother, the son, the disciple.

• The two people, the new mother and the new son, are the only central actors in the Gospel who remain anonymous. Because they almost always appear in association with named actors, we must suppose that the narrator consciously chose not to name them. No one knows the name of the beloved disciple; and if we had only this Gospel, the same thing could be said of the mother. The anonymous status makes it probable that the narrator viewed them in their representative character.[2]

• Throughout the Gospel, familial terms ordinarily carry symbolic weight: father, son, brothers, children. It would be strange if that were not true in this instance.

• The only result of the episode that is mentioned is the action of the disciple; special interest, therefore, is drawn to that action. It would seem to have unusual importance for both narrator and readers in the period after Easter. In some way that feature in the story was designed to change their attitude or actions.[3]

In view of all these observations we must try to grasp the symbolic reverberations of the story. And that impels us to explore elsewhere in the Gospel the roles of these two representative figures.

The mother appears on the Johannine stage only twice— once near the beginning and again near the end. (The oblique reference to her in 6:42 is no exception.) Both episodes are so elliptical that no certain interpretation is possible. It seems probable, however, that when the narrator reported the first incident he had the later one in mind. Both stories (2:1–5; 19:26–27) follow an announcement of the appearance of Jesus as the "King of Israel" (1:49; 19:19–22). Both are oriented toward the arrival of Jesus' hour (in the first it had not come; in the second it had fully come). In both, Jesus' glory is manifested. In both, the mother is addressed rather bluntly as woman *(gunai);* in both, the presence of a disciple is significant. These things being true, the scene "on the third day" may help us discern some of the symbolic nuances of the final meeting.

Three things are surely important clues in the first incident: the wedding, the feast, the need for wine.[4] All three have overtones. Israel had often been characterized as the bride of Yahweh (Hosea 2:16–20; Jeremiah 2:2, 32; Ezekiel 16:8–63). The dawn of the messianic age had been compared to a wedding feast (Isaiah 25:6–8; 55:1–5; Proverbs 9:1–6; Psalm 23:5), in which many guests join in the joy of the bridegroom. So the provision of wine for that feast, out of stone jars used customarily for "Jewish rites of purification," became a sign of messianic glory, the fulfillment of God's promises to Israel.

Within such a setting the narrator introduces Jesus' mother. She seems to have been there before the arrival of Jesus and his disciples; this suggests that in some sense she was their host. Her words "they have no wine" imply that she had accepted some responsibility for the feast itself. We may well ask whether these words also imply that she unconsciously anticipated what would happen when the hour had fully come. Was this an unwitting prophecy? It is possible. When the hour of this son comes he will want to provide wine for the messianic feast and he will have the authority for doing just that. It is curious that she should disappear from the scene as soon as she has issued her command to the servants, "Do whatever he tells you." In this command she becomes instrumental in calling for this first "sign" of the son's glory. The unmet thirst of the messianic people is linked through her words to the power of this messiah to quench it. Thus we may perceive both in her statement to her son and in her command to the servants a prophetic anticipation of the coming fulfillment of Israel's need for the Messiah. In this respect it would seem that the narrator is more concerned with her representative role than with her individual story.

In response to her tacit appeal, Jesus speaks impersonally, if not brutally: "Woman, what have you to do with me? My hour has not yet come [2:4]." It sounds as if Jesus did not want at this time to recognize any filial relation. Not until his hour has come will he acknowledge any direct bond, and then his concern will be not with his own "family" but with a new "family" to be formed around this woman and his disciple as a nucleus. There is a sharp contrast between his two rejoinders:

"Woman, what have you to do with me?"

"Woman, look! This is your son!"

Such a contrast is surely related to the nearness of his hour. In that hour the relation denied in the first episode will be affirmed and a new relationship established.

In this dramatic story it is on the cross that Jesus takes the initiative in establishing a new family tie between two anonymous figures who represent larger communities. Whom, then, does the woman represent? She participates in the drama as the community that has given birth to this Messiah. She stands at this strategic moment as the Israel to whom God has fulfilled the promise. We should recall that the scripture had traditionally spoken of God's people in the feminine gender. Certainty is beyond reach, but B. Olsson seems near the mark when he writes that this woman represents "that part of the people of God which really is faithful to its tradition and its faith, those who believe in Moses and the Scriptures and are thereby the link between the old and the new."[5]

To her from the cross, as part of his final work, the Messiah discloses the identity of her new son. It is more than an introduction; implicitly, it is God's command: "You must recognize this disciple as your son." (The verb describing the action of the disciple, *lambano*, is probably the action prescribed for the mother as well. It means to receive, to accept, to acknowledge as one's own.[6])

If this identification seems cogent, the prophetic revelation of God's will for the messianic people conveys an appeal for her to respond positively to the continuing mission of the community of disciples. This is the moment when the first son's work is finished and the new son's work is beginning; it is also the moment of fulfillment of that initial prophecy that anticipated the entire conflict: "He came to his own home, and his own people received him not, but to all who received him, he gave power to become children of God [1:11–12])." From the first word of the

Baptist to the last word of the Messiah, the messianic community has been divided between rejection and acceptance. On the cross the Messiah refuses to accept failure (in a way not unlike the example of Paul [Romans 11:28f.]). He announces a final revelatory word to his mother: "Accept this disciple (and his community) as your son. My mission continues in his; he now is your son." It is perhaps significant that the narrator does not give her response; this may be because his readers confront a messianic people that is still deeply divided.

So we turn to examine the second manifesto in this enigmatic conversation: "Look! This is your mother!" This word was obviously framed to parallel the first word, yet there is an imbalance between them. In coming second, this word receives a greater emphasis. Only to this word is a response specified. Only in this case are we dealing with an actor who had appeared frequently in the preceding chapters. The story has established a closer bond between Jesus and this disciple than with the mother. Moreover, this disciple not only represents the whole company of believers, but he is also closely linked to those congregations for which John is writing.

We should look at some of these points more closely. This disciple was first introduced to the readers at the beginning of the Farewell Address as the disciple who was trusted by Jesus with secret knowledge (13:23). Thereafter he remained a central witness to the key events, moving from the supper table, to the court of the high priest, to the cross, to the empty tomb, to the fishing expedition, to the final verses in which he was recognized as the source of the traditions on which this Gospel was based. In important ways he had become Jesus' alter ego, his appointee to serve as spokesman after Jesus' death. His relation to Jesus was characterized in three ways: as the disciple whom Jesus loved, as the one who sat "close to the breast" of his master, and as one to whom Jesus had seemed to promise survival until his return. The designation "close to the breast" is significant, because the same phrase was used to describe Jesus' own relation to God. The phrase signifies not only personal affection and intimacy but also knowledge of the mind and will of God, along with the obligation to share that knowledge with the community. As Jesus was God's beloved spokesman, so this man was Jesus' beloved spokesman and, as such, fully qualified to be present at the cross, where he could receive and execute Jesus' final bequest.[7]

Simultaneously, this anonymous figure clearly represented the band of disciples, often speaking to them and for them. It was as a leader of the disciples that he could recognize Jesus' presence on the beach, after a night of fruitless fishing. It was as a recipient of the Paraclete that he could transmit all that Jesus had taught and done. As we have already observed, the Johannine community probably traced its existence to his own work among them; thus they would assume that in speaking to him Jesus had them in mind as well.

We add one other note about the symbolic identity of this disciple. He may have been present in the high priest's courtyard on the occasion of the final interrogation of Jesus (18:15f.). If so, he seems to have been known and respected as a person (possibly even a friend) known to Caiaphas. By speaking to the doorkeeper he could gain admittance for Peter. This connection may also be suggested by his presence at the cross, something that is in itself unusual in the case of criminal executions. If so, this man could serve as a triple link: between Jesus and his disciples, between those disciples and John's readers, and between the entire band of believers and the official establishment of "the Jews."

It is that complex role that gives to his action at the cross its potential significance. Only his action is described, an action that forms the climax of the episode: "So from that hour on, the disciple took her to his own [19:27]." He acted as if Jesus' word had been a command, and the story is told as if his action represented an intended completion of Jesus' own work, a continuation, in fact, of that "hour" of revelation and redemption. What, then, did his action signify to John and his first readers? Any effort to translate symbolic actions into verbal equivalents is, of course, doomed to failure. When symbolic richness is reduced to prosaic banalities much is lost. Surely, however, we must conclude that the disciple's action in acknowledging this mother as his own was in line with the intent of the Crucified. Can we also infer that such an action on the part of the disciple was far from easy? It must have represented a miraculous reversal to make it an appropriate sequel to the crucifixion.

If the phrase "his own" *(ta idia)* refers not to the disciple's own home, in the sense of his individual place of residence, but to "the deeper family," "his own sheep," those who belong to Christ,[8] the Christian congregations to which John was writing, the dimensions of the miracle begin to emerge. Now the command of Jesus is addressed through the disciple to those congregations. And the disciple's action is translated into an action to be confirmed by them. They are ordered to acknowledge and to welcome Jesus' mother (i.e., the messianic community of Israel) into their own fellowship. They must continue to seek reconciliation with their enemies in synagogues and temple. They must refuse to despair of the ultimate success of that mission. "From that hour" they must obey this word as the command of their king: "Look! This is your mother!" The exclamation points are entirely justified. The obedience of the beloved disciple makes obligatory the same obedience on the part of the community that traces its origin to him. In their action of hospitality the past history of God's people becomes reconciled to its future history. This is not an idle dream. This is what happened in the hour of Jesus' death. This is an index to the power released by that death. The beloved disciple welcomed the Messiah's beloved mother into the community of those reborn as God's children. The word of the Crucified cancels out anti-Semitism among his disciples by means of a pro-Semitic command, an inescapable "Love your enemies." This word of the Messiah cancels out the brutality of his first word to his mother: "What have you to do with me? My hour has not yet come [2:4]." After Jesus' hour had come she had a new son and his disciple(s) had a new mother.

We should not fail to note, in returning to the literary context in chapters 19 and 20, the sequence of four prophetic calls: Pilate's call to the Jews to recognize their king; Jesus' call for his mother to recognize her new son and for his disciple to recognize his new mother; and Jesus' message to his disciples concerning their Father: "I am ascending to my Father and your Father." Now for the first time those disciples are recognized by Jesus as brothers (20:17).[9] The circle of family metaphors is complete in these recognition scenes: father, mother, son, brothers. God's work reaches its culmination in the creation of a new family and its reconciliation with the old. The scene at the cross celebrates that reconciliation, for it closes the circle of the beloveds: the beloved son sent to the beloved world, the beloved disciple reconciled to the beloved mother. Many of the symbolic meanings of the scene at the cross elude recapture in words, but there is much in the disciple's obedience in welcoming the new mother that carried profound nuances to those whom the narrator included among "his own," namely, his readers.

We may add this note. Quite often in the Bible we find two female figures being used as images of the elect community: the marital and the maternal.[10] Both bride and mother become familiar actors in the apocalyptic drama; both are prominent in the book of Revelation. In this respect the role of the anonymous mother in John 2 and 19 is similar to the role of the anonymous mother of Revelation 12. In both cases she fulfills a heavenly design associated with the death of the Messiah; in both cases she becomes the mother of the Messiah's followers. The mother of one becomes the mother of all.*

In a poignant scene in Dostoevsky's *Brothers Karamazov* there is a dialogue between God and the Virgin Mary. God "points to the hands and feet of her son, nailed to the cross, and asks, 'How can I forgive his tormentors?' "[12] The implications are obvious. God is an omnipotent judge whose deadly wrath has been aroused by the dastardly deeds of the Jews. To forgive those tormentors is beyond the realm of possibility; justice forbids it. It requires the intercessions of the Virgin to turn aside the divine wrath. Unfortunately, this dialogue reflects a deeply entrenched tradition in Christian thought. The Johannine picture of the crucifixion is almost totally different. Here the mercy of God, God's love for the world, flows through the crucified

---

*The maternal image should perhaps be extended to a more remote affiliation to the role of Eve. Still another possible affiliation is to the role of Rachel, wife of Jacob/Israel (cf. Matthew 2:18) and mother of Benjamin. In this latter connection it is possible that John shaped the image of the beloved disciple into accordance with the portrait of Benjamin in Deuteronomy 33:12.[11]

Son and through the Son's persecuted disciples in a mission to their enemies. That mission is made possible by these words from the cross in which the son discloses a new family bond between mother and disciple, the old and the new messianic communities now united in response to his disclosure and demand.

Chapter XV

FEED MY SHEEP

As a pastor, I am obliged by divine command to give my life for those whom I love—and that is for all Salvadorans, even for those who may assassinate me. If the threats should come to pass I offer God, for this very moment, my blood for the redemption and resurrection of El Salvador.[1]

A declaration by Korean Christians: "We should prepare ourselves for martyrdom, if necessary, as our forefathers did."[2]

We have been seeking throughout these chapters to become temporary residents of the Johannine community and to understand the successive messages addressed to such people by the risen Lord. We have observed that these residents may be divided into two groups: believers and their charismatic leaders. Although all stories in the Gospel held interest for both groups, members of the two groups would read different segments of the story with differing degrees of empathy. For example, in reading the intercessions of Jesus in chapter 17, leaders who were undergoing the rigors of persecution would find greater relevance in the petitions of 17:7–19; rank-and-file believers would identify themselves more easily with the less urgent petitions of 17:20–26. In the account of the crucifixion itself, believers might feel greater affinity with the roles of Joseph, Nicodemus, and the soldier; leaders might sense a greater kinship with the commands addressed by Jesus to his mother and to his beloved disciple.

The stories of the post-Easter appearances seem to be oriented, with possibly two exceptions, toward the charismatic leaders. At least in chapter 20 the disciples hold the center of the stage. It is to them that the Lord appears. He breathes the Spirit on them and sends them out with his authority to forgive sins. They do not proceed with their assignments until they have seen him, until he has banished their fears, until they have heard his words: "I am sending you." It is probably significant that the signs are done "in the presence of the *disciples*." It was, in fact, one of the necessary qualifications of a prophet to see "special demonstrations of the character and power of God,"[3] to hear the voice of the ascended Lord, and receive the command: "Go . . . Tell!"

It was not necessary for all believers to have such visions, auditions, and commissions. So the first exception comes at the end of chapter 20, when the narrator relays the Lord's blessing on all who believe without seeing what Thomas and the others had seen. It was enough for believers to hear the testimonies of their Spirit-controlled leaders. And in the case of John's readers it was enough to have his book (20:31).*

In chapter 21 the narrator turns back to stories that would be of prime concern to disciples. In these stories the spotlight no longer falls on their installation or authorization, but on their later work as Jesus' messengers. The narrator relies on two traditional metaphorical complexes to describe their work: They now serve as fishermen and as shepherds. In both cases the perspectives are fairly obvious. Their first role is that of fishermen, of whom there are seven in all, with Peter and the beloved disciple as the leaders. Although the unbroken net and the catch of fish have symbolic significance,[5] the heavier accent falls on the role of the seven fishermen, with a strong contrast between earlier futility and later success, and a corresponding

---

*In the *you* of 20:31 the narrator addresses his readers as those who have believed without seeing. The contrasts between them and Thomas are important. He did not accept the testimony of eyewitnesses; they do. He had been a member of the twelve; they are not. He demanded sight before believing; they could not. He had direct access to Jesus' presence; they did not, yet they could and did receive life in his name.[4]

contrast between the night and the day. Those contrasts coincide with the absence and presence of Jesus, a presence that is marked by obedience to his instructions on where to cast their net. The charismatic leaders in John's churches would be stupid indeed to miss the relevance of this story to their vocation, insofar as that vocation included the process of bringing unbelievers into the community of faith. Among other implications the story suggests that any success in that work becomes evidence of the resurrection of Jesus. On bringing their nets to land they would themselves receive a welcome from the Lord.

After breakfast Jesus initiates a conversation with Simon, son of John, in which the work of shepherds becomes the key metaphor. The story unfolds in such a way as to make the story of Peter relevant to all successor shepherds. The risen Lord asks them the same question, with its repeated emphasis, and issues the same command as a test of their faithfulness. This metaphor complex brings into play many dimensions in the biblical imagery. Unlike the fishing complex, this metaphor is more applicable to a leader's care for believers, men and women and children who already belong to God's flock.

Not only is this conversation appropriate to the work of later shepherds, it is also suitable as the culmination of all the earlier incidents in which Simon Peter had been onstage. If we take the Gospel as a whole, the part played by this disciple constitutes one of the threads that links the beginning to the end.

But can we take the Gospel as a whole, including this last "follow me"? According to the majority of scholars today, we neither can nor should view this final episode as part of the original Gospel. It is one of their firm convictions that chapter 21 is an addition to the original document, an epilogue or an appendix probably added by a later redactor. This consensus is based on two key convictions: first, that the three verses at the end of chapter 20 were designed to serve as the conclusion of the entire Gospel; second, that chapter 21, as an additional resurrection appearance, is too loosely related to the preceding chapters to have come from the same author. My own study of the Gospel fails to support this majority opinion, for I have found abundant evidence that the narrator intended from the beginning to end the story where he did. Although my full argument need not be given here,[6] I must rely on it in discussing the stories of the two leading disciples.

However the debate on chapter 21 may turn out, without this chapter the story of Peter would be incomplete. The narrator has given him too much attention to allow him to disappear from the scene at 20:10. The story itself is extremely colorful and provocative. Between its beginning and its end there is a striking symmetry, the narrator introducing him in 1:41 and dismissing him in 21:22. In both chapters he is introduced to the Lord by another disciple (1:41; 21:7). Early in the story he appears as spokesman for the twelve (6:68), and it is at his invitation that the group goes fishing (21:3).

It is during the supper in the upper room, however, that the narrator gives major attention to this portrait. Here we note three separate scenes, each with strong allusive and predictive overtones. The first deals with the highly symbolic action of Jesus in washing the disciples' feet. To Peter's initial refusal Jesus replies: "What I am doing you do not know now, but afterward you will understand [13:7]." After what? Almost certainly after Jesus' death. This is more than a matter of simple timing. The implication is clear that it is by Jesus' death that cleansing will take place. Only after that cleansing will Peter comprehend what had happened earlier. Only then will he (with the other disciples and their successors) come to know what it means to emulate the Master's example by washing one another's feet. By implication this dialogue is prophetic of the coming self-sacrifice of Jesus, of the knowledge that will be conveyed by that "washing," and of their subsequent discovery that only self-sacrifice can embody the truth that no messenger of Jesus can claim to be greater than his Master (13:16). That is the prophecy that is supported by his authoritative blessing: "Blessed are you if you do them." But such a blessing will not take effect in advance of that obedience; the first episode in which that obedience is reported of Peter comes in chapter 21. Then Jesus' example will be validated by Peter's example. Then, at last, Peter will join "the order of the towel."

This conversation with Peter is dovetailed into Jesus' warnings about the coming betrayal (13:11, 18, 21f.). Although Jesus reiterates those warnings and the narrator neatly contrasts Jesus' act of hospitality and the act of Judas by which hospitality is denied, Peter bespeaks the ignorance of all of them, "Who is it?" Peter's ignorance is not dispelled by Jesus' answer. "No one at the table knew . . ." It is the Lord and not his disciples who can predict where treason will strike. And none of the disciples escapes some complicity in that treason. Again the narrator is deftly preparing the readers for later scenes in which all the warnings and blessings will come true.

The third prediction at the supper table reveals what was only implicit in the other two. The departure of Jesus is at hand, and the only question at issue is where he is going (cf. above, chapter X). To that question John's readers know the answer: He is going to the Father by way of the cross. That has been his destination from the beginning. In this case, Jesus makes a double assertion: Now you are unable to follow me; afterward you will follow (13:36–38). Peter ignores the second and concentrates on the first. Why is he unable to follow now? After all, he is ready to give his life for Jesus. Readers have little difficulty in understanding this interchange. Peter was mistaken about where Jesus was going, mistaken about Jesus' death, mistaken about his own readiness to follow. Accordingly, the Master replies with his magisterial revelation, "Truly, truly I say . . . ," and within a few hours that prediction is fulfilled. The first prediction of Jesus is the clue to the narrator's arrangement of chapter 18, which makes it doubly clear why Peter is unable to follow now. By his swordplay in the garden he tried to prevent Jesus from drinking the Father's cup. In his efforts to keep Jesus from being handed over to the Jews, he unwittingly served their king and another kingdom (18:36). That proved to be a form of treason only a little less culpable, if at all, than Judas'. Peter proved himself unable to follow and thus fully carried out Jesus' expectation that he would deny that he had been in the garden with Jesus. He would warm himself at the fire of the enemies. As soon as he had denied Jesus three times, the cock crowed (13:38; 18:27). The exact correlation between prediction and event is clearly intended.

But what about the second part of Jesus' assertion: "You shall follow afterward"? Where is the sequel to that assertion to be found? It would be curious indeed if a narrator who had taken such pains to tell the first half of the story should fail to tell its second half. Surely we do not find the sequel in Peter's momentary appearance at the tomb, in response to Mary's confused summons (20:2). There is no inkling of Peter's believing, nor do his actions represent any kind of following.[7] Furthermore, the narrator makes no mention of Peter's presence with the other disciples when the Lord came and stood among them (20:19–29). The only fulfillment of Jesus' second assertion about Peter is to be found in the breakfast dialogue with Jesus in chapter 21. We can only assume that the narrator crafted these three stories simultaneously: the double prophecy in chapter 13, the fulfillment of the first half in chapter 18, and the fulfillment of the second half in chapter 21.

The contrast between the night in the garden and the breakfast on the beach is sharp and clear. But there are even greater correspondences between the predictions at the supper and the fulfillments described on the beach. In both texts the accent falls on following Jesus. In both, such following required the sacrifice of life, by which God is glorified. In both, this following, this sacrifice, is an expression of the disciple's love for his master. There is even a precise mathematical correspondence: the prediction of a threefold denial (13:38) is fulfilled in those three fear-ridden denials in the courtyard of the high priest, while that *now* is replaced by an *afterward* in which Jesus questions Peter three times, Peter replies three times, and then Jesus issues the same command three times. The supper is followed by breakfast; the denials that took place just before dawn are replaced by the pledges of obedience just after dawn.

Jesus is concerned with "my sheep," a phrase that by implication accepts Jesus as shepherd (cp. 10:1–18). Jesus makes Peter his successor as a shepherd, whose primary concern must be the feeding of the one flock. And we cannot be far wrong to think of Peter as the model for his own successors, whose love for an apparently absent Jesus must also take the form of faithful care of Jesus' people. The story indicates that love = feeding and feeding = following. It indicates something more, something that injects iron into those three platitudes. By his parenthetical comment in 21:19 the narrator makes sure that none of his readers fails to notice that in Peter's case, to follow did mean martyrdom. So the threefold question about Peter's love is translated into a threefold command to feed the flock; that command, in turn, is defined by following, which, in turn, is defined by martyrdom. Just as "the prophet like Moses" had fed the flock by giving his flesh "for the life of the world [6:51]," so too would Peter feed the lambs by his death.

If we may visualize prophets in John's churches who thought of themselves as successors of Peter, this story from beginning to end would convey multiple cautions and encouragements. For them, the end of the story in chapter 21 would throw much light on the otherwise enigmatic discussion about foot washing. It would help to suggest many allegorical and typological details in the teaching concerning the good shepherd, the stranger from whom the sheep flee, the wolves who kill the sheep, the hired servants who flee at the first approach of wolves, and true shepherds who, because they know the Father, lay down their lives for the sheep (10:1–18). John's readers would be able to identify each group in terms of their own work. So too Peter's story has become for them a recent edition of the parable of the seed falling into the earth and of the symbolic analogy of the vine and its fruitful branches (15:1–20). In all these Johannine narratives we are justified in finding anticipations of the work of Peter, as well as symbolic equivalents of the laconic confession of the apostle Paul: "Death is at work in us, but life is at work in you [2 Cor. 4:12]."

The narrator uses the end of Peter's story to introduce another matter in which he has a special interest: the post-Easter work of the beloved disciple. This concern is injected into the discussion by Peter after he had learned of his own impending martyrdom: "Lord, what about this man?"

The insertion of this question reflects a strong interest on the part of the narrator; he is unwilling to end his book without including an appropriate reference to the destiny of that disciple. If he had finished his account at 20:31, the final appearance of this disciple would have been at the tomb (20:10), and that would have been a strange conclusion for one who had held a privileged position at the Supper, who had been entrusted with Jesus' secret knowledge, who had been given responsibility for the Messiah's mother. Viewed simply as a literary artist, the narrator would have been guilty of great clumsiness had he given such prominence to a character without indicating the outcome.

The injection of this question also probably reflects an interest on the part of John's audience, for they felt a stronger bond to this disciple than to Peter. As we have noted, it is likely that this disciple "functioned as the founder within the Johannine community."[8] The earlier episodes also suggest that certain tensions had developed among various Christian flocks over the comparative merits of their several shepherds, some congregations partial to Peter and others to the beloved disciple. Such tensions may explain why the two disciples often appear in the same scenes, and why in those scenes the beloved disciple is usually cast in a better light (13:21–26; 18:15–18; 20:2–8; 21:7–8). It is typical of Peter that he should misunderstand or reject the Master's lessons, but this is not true of his fellow shepherd. By the time this Gospel appeared, readers knew that Peter had been executed (21:18) and that his colleague had died from so-called natural causes. Perhaps this contrast added acid to the invidious comparisons being drawn between the two shepherds on the part of their supporting congregations. These are all conjectures, of course, but they are encouraged by the question that Peter raised: "Lord, what about this man [21:21]?" (Why should one shepherd suffer more than another?)

To ignore the answer of Jesus is all too easy, because that answer seems to have lost its cogency to later readers. Three observations, however, may indicate its original importance. First, it is the final word of the risen Lord that is recorded in the Gospel. As such, it is unlikely to have been a casual remark of little significance for the life of John's churches. Second, this message is addressed *to* one of the two leaders of the first generation *about* the fate of the second of those heroes. Third, it is a message dealing with an issue that looms large in any minority religious community that is undergoing severe persecution from a majority religious community: Why is one leader killed and not another? Does the fact of extreme self-sacrifice validate the leadership of one and invalidate the leadership of another? Once the issue is posed in such realistic terms, the strategic importance of Jesus' answer will become obvious: "If it is my will that he remain until I come, what is that to you? Follow me [21:22]!"[9]

In the words "what is that to you?" we may detect the last of several rebukes given to Peter in the Gospel. But in the days of the narrator this is a rebuke issued to a shepherd who has glorified God with his death as a martyr. This means, among other things, that the narrator intends the rebuke to be heard not by Peter but by successor shepherds and their supporters. To him, the final command from their Lord prohibits invidious comparisons among leaders, comparisons based on different degrees of self-sacrifice. Each shepherd has only one duty—to follow—and that duty makes irrelevant what happens to other shepherds.

A second accent emerges in the words "if it is my will." It is the will of the transcendent Lord that determines the end of the vocation of each of his appointees. Enemies may think that they hold that power in their hands. Christians may suppose that martyrs are more or less devoted (or wise, or effective) than non-martyrs. No, it is the will of the Lord that determines the varying outcomes. To follow him is to trust his will. Here the basic message is not very different from Paul's warning to a divided community in Rome: "Who are you to pass judgment on the servant of another? It is before his own master that he stands or falls [Rom. 14:4]."

So we may be entirely confident that the narrator had good reasons for ending his Gospel with this message from the risen Lord. We may be less confident that we can recover those reasons. As I have said, one of those reasons may have been his desire to end the debates among Christians over the relative merits of shepherds who lose or do not lose their lives in line of duty. Another of those reasons is this: He may have wanted to terminate his story with a reference to the work of the beloved disciple, whose faithful witness as a non-martyr here received the imprimatur of the Lord's will. If so, this reason comes to the surface in a closing parenthetical comment by the narrator: "This is the disciple who is bearing witness to these things, and who has written these things; and we know that his testimony [*martyria*] is true [21:24]."

With this verse the focus of the narrator's interest shifts

away from the charismatic leaders of his churches *toward* the believers in those churches. (This is the second exception that I mentioned earlier, on p. 154.) I believe that the narrator wanted to terminate his story with the work of this disciple because those believers have been dependent on his testimony. Now those believers can know that the death of this witness had also been willed by the risen Lord. They can now be confident that Jesus had loved this disciple and been loved by him to the very end. He too had fulfilled the earlier promise of Jesus: "He who has my commandments and keeps them, he it is who loves me; and he who loves me will be loved by my Father, and I will love him and manifest myself to him. . . . We will come to him and make our home with him [14:21, 23]." The closing dialogue between Jesus and Peter, with its reference to this other disciple, provided the narrator with an opportunity to trace the traditions on which his readers were dependent, back through his own witness, through the witness of the beloved disciple, to the final verification by the witness of the risen Lord.

Moreover, this vindication by the risen Lord had itself been instigated by Peter's query. It had been Peter who had first introduced this disciple at the supper table when Jesus had first predicted Judas' betrayal. It had also been Peter who had introduced this disciple into the empty tomb, with its ambiguous testimony, and Peter who had initiated the fishing expedition, with its night time futility and morning success. Now at the end it is Peter who raised the question about the other shepherd's fate. This, in turn, elicited the final judgment by the risen Lord on a shepherd who had not been martyred. That shepherd had also followed his Lord; his work had fulfilled the Master's will. Thus the Gospel put its readers into direct touch with both Peter and the beloved disciple and through them into touch with the victorious martyr, Jesus. The links between the sheep of the flock, their shepherds, and the Good Shepherd were as strong as God could make them.

Notes

Introduction

1. Cited by David E. Aune, *The Cultic Setting of Realized Eschatology in Early Christianity* (Leiden: Brill, 1972), p. 47, n. 1.

Part One: The Character of the Conversation

1. G. Stade, *New York Times*, Book Review Section, May 27, 1979.

Chapter I. The Narrator

1. John V. Taylor, *The Go-Between God* (Philadelphia: Fortress Press, 1973), p. 75.

2. In this and the following chapter I have used some material that first appeared in my essay "The Audience of the Fourth Evangelist," *Interpretation* 31 (1977):339–54, and in J.L. Mays, *Interpreting the Gospels* (Philadelphia: Fortress Press, 1981), pp. 247–64.

3. Marinus de Jonge, *Jesus: Stranger from Heaven and Son of God* (Missoula, MT: Scholars Press, 1977), p. 12.

4. Joachim Jeremias, *New Testament Theology* (New York: Scribner's, 1971), 2:52.

5. M. Eugene Boring, *Sayings of the Risen Jesus* (New York: Cambridge University Press, 1982), pp. 19, 48–50, 260–61.

6. Ibid., p. 16; similar definitions may be found in David Aune, *The Cultic Setting of Realized Eschatology in Early Christianity* (Leiden: Brill, 1972), pp. 69ff., and in David Hill, *New Testament Prophecy* (Atlanta: John Knox Press, 1980), pp. 4–9.

7. Boring, op. cit., p. 76.

8. Gerd Theissen, *The Sociology of Early Palestinian Christianity*, trans. John Bowden (Philadelphia: Fortress Press, 1978), p. 7.

9. Aune, op. cit., p. 101.

10. George B. Caird, *The Language and Imagery of the Bible* (Philadelphia: Westminster Press, 1980), p. 237.

11. B. Olsson, *Structure and Meaning in the Fourth Gospel* (Lund: Gleerup, 1974), pp. 279ff.; Boring, op. cit., pp. 95f.

12. Olsson, op. cit., pp. 262ff.

13. In this paragraph I have used material from R. Alan Culpepper, "The Narrator and the Farewell Discourse in John," pp. 4–5; typescript. Cf. also R. Alan Culpepper, "The Narrator in the Fourth Gospel," Society of Biblical Literature, Seminar Papers (Chico, CA: Scholars Press, 1982), p. 90.

14. Caird, op. cit., p. 211.
15. U. Simon, *Story and Faith* (London: SPCK, 1975), p. 80.
16. Olsson, op. cit., p. 179.
17. Culpepper, "Farewell Discourse," op. cit., p. 15; also "Narrator in the Fourth Gospel," op. cit., p. 89.
18. Rudolf Schnackenburg, *The Gospel According to St. John* (New York: Herder, 1968), 2:23.

Chapter II. The First Readers
1. Samuel Terrien, *The Elusive Presence*, ed. Ruth N. Anshen (New York: Harper & Row, 1978), p. 142.
2. J. Louis Martyn, *History and Theology in the Fourth Gospel* (New York: Harper & Row, 1968), p. xviii.
3. Morris L. West, *The Clowns of God* (New York: William Morrow, 1981), frontispiece.
4. David E. Aune, *The Cultic Setting of Realized Eschatology in Early Christianity* (Leiden: Brill, 1972), p. 103.
5. An extended discussion of these twin gifts may be found in Paul S. Minear, *New Testament Apocalyptic* (Nashville: Abingdon Press, 1981), chaps. 1 and 2; see also M. Eugene Boring, *Sayings of the Risen Jesus* (New York: Cambridge University Press, 1982), p. 64.
6. A survey of the evidence for the portrait of Jesus as a prophet like Moses may be found in Wayne A. Meeks, *The Prophet-King* (Leiden: Brill, 1967).
7. Paul S. Minear, "The Audience of the Fourth Evangelist," *Interpretation* 31 (1977):341ff.
8. Marinus de Jonge, *Jesus: Stranger from Heaven and Son of God* (Missoula: MT: Scholars Press, 1977), p. 6.
9. Rudolf Bultmann, *The Gospel of John* (Philadelphia: Westminster Press, 1971), pp. 69f., 512.
10. John Milton, *Paradise Lost*, XII, lines 478–85.
11. Meeks, op. cit., pp. 69ff.
12. Paul S. Minear, "Jesus' Audiences According to Luke," *Novum Testamentum* 16 (1974):81–109.
13. Paul S. Minear, "Audience Criticism and Markan Ecclesiology," in H. Baltensweiler and B. Reicke, eds., *Neues Testament und Geschichte* (Zurich: Theologische Verlag, 1972), pp. 79–90.
14. Paul S. Minear, "The Disciples and Crowds in the Gospel of Matthew," *Anglican Theological Review*, Suppl. Series 3 (March 1974):28–44.
15. Burnett H. Streeter, *The Four Gospels* (New York: Macmillan, 1925), p. 367.
16. "The Johannine community contained a significant group of

Christian prophets among its leaders" [Boring, op. cit., p. 48]; for the negative view, cf. C.K. Barrett, *The Gospel According to St. John* (Philadelphia: Westminster Press, 1978), p. 57.

17. The Farewell Address of Jesus exemplifies a pattern that is found in many biblical passages. It contains six elements: a farewell to friends, a recall of past associations, an exhortation to faithfulness, a prediction of the future, the appointment of successors, and a blessing or a prayer for them. Cf. J.F. Randall, "The Theme of Unity in John 17:20–23," *Ephemerides Theologicae Lovanienses* 41 (1965):376.

Chapter III. The Adversaries

1. Gerald Brenan, *Thoughts in a Dry Season* (New York: Cambridge University Press, 1978), p. 53.

2. Paul S. Minear, "To Ask and To Receive," in D.Y. Hadidian, ed., *Intergerini Parietis Septum* (Pittsburgh: Pickwick Press, 1981), pp. 239f.

3. Raymond E. Brown, *The Gospel According to John* (New York: Doubleday, 1970), 2:702.

4. Barnabas Lindars, *The Gospel of John* (London: Oliphants, 1972), p. 497.

5. Jurgen Moltmann, *The Crucified God* (New York: Harper & Row, 1973), p. 37.

6. B. Olsson, *Structure and Meaning in the Fourth Gospel* (Lund: Gleerup, 1974), pp. 146f.

7. Peder Borgen, *Bread from Heaven* (Leiden: Brill, 1965), pp. 177f.; see also S. Pancaro, *The Law in the Fourth Gospel* (Leiden: Brill, 1975), pp. 288f.

8. Rudolf Bultmann observes that in 18:20 the phrase "to the world" was equivalent to the phrase "to you," but he does nothing to draw out the far-reaching implications of that equation (*The Gospel of John* [Philadelphia: Westminster Press, 1971], p. 646).

9. As Bultmann observes, "Pilate by no means represents the world in the same way as the Jews and their rulers [op. cit., p. 647]."

10. Walker Percy, *The Second Coming* (New York: Farrar, Straus & Giroux, 1980), pp. 271f.

Chapter IV. The Objectives

1. Morris L. West, *The Clowns of God* (New York: William Morrow, 1981), p. 93.

2. David E. Aune, *The Cultic Setting of Realized Eschatology in Early Christianity* (Leiden: Brill, 1972), pp. 78ff.

3. Wayne A. Meeks, *The Prophet-King* (Leiden: Brill, 1967), pp. 294ff.

4. Marinus de-Jonge, *Jesus: Stranger from Heaven and Son of God* (Missoula, MT: Scholars Press, 1977), p. 148.

5. J. Louis Martyn, *History and Theology in the Fourth Gospel* (New York: Harper & Row, 1968), p. 91.

6. "The central violent contradiction between the primitive Christian kerygma and the Jewish Messianic hope is that which sets the crucified Messiah of Christian experience over against the triumphant hero of Jewish fancy [T.W. Manson, *The Servant-Messiah* (New York: Cambridge University Press, 1953), p. 36]."

7. Meeks, op. cit., pp. 67–68, 80.

8. George B. Caird, *The Language and Imagery of the Bible* (Philadelphia: Westminster Press, 1980), pp. 159f.

Chapter V. The Time Frame

1. This saying has been attributed to C.S. Lewis, but I have been unable to locate its origin.

2. W.H. Brownlee, in J.H. Charlesworth, ed., *John and Qumran* (London: Chapman, 1972), p. 184.

3. B. Olsson, *Structure and Meaning in the Fourth Gospel* (Lund: Gleerup, 1974), p. 288.

4. John A.T. Robinson, *Redating the New Testament* (London: SCM Press, 1976), p. 263.

5. Peder Borgen, *Bread from Heaven* (Leiden: Brill, 1965), pp. 1, 21, 45, 147f.

6. Olsson, op. cit., p. 286; David E. Aune, *The Cultic Setting of Realized Eschatology in Early Christianity* (Leiden: Brill, 1972), pp. 105–35.

7. Matthias Rissi, *New Testament Studies* 29 (1983):48–54.

8. S. Pancaro, *The Law in the Fourth Gospel* (Leiden: Brill, 1975), p. 496.

9. C.H. Dodd, in *Neotestamentica et Patristica, Novum Testamentum,* Suppl. vol. 6 (Leiden: Brill, 1962), p. 138.

10. Ibid., p. 140. It is true that Dodd attributed this attitude not to the Evangelist but to one of his hypothetical sources. However, it seems curious for the Evangelist to place so much dramatic weight on this scene if this climactic saying did not represent his own attitude. The key statement "that Jesus should die for the nation" is entirely typical of the narrator's editorial comments as sprinkled throughout the Gospel.

11. Robinson, op. cit., p. 282.

12. J. Louis Martyn, *History and Theology in the Fourth Gospel* (New York: Harper & Row, 1968), pp. 18–41.

13. Ibid., p. 18.

14. Ibid., p. 20.

15. A summary of recent discussions of the matter of dating may be found in Robert Kysar, *The Fourth Evangelist and His Gospel* (Minneapolis: Augsburg, 1975), pp. 167ff.

16. John "could be an interpretation of the life of Jesus written by a cultured Christian Jew of Judea during the late 50's or early 60's [Olsson, op. cit., p. 289, n. 73]."

Part Two: Messages from a Victorious Martyr
1. John Donne, *Complete English Poems* (London: Penguin, n.d.), p. 326.
2. M. Eugene Boring, *Sayings of the Risen Jesus* (New York: Cambridge University Press, 1982), p. 8.

Chapter VI. My Peace I Give to You
1. Arthur Koestler, *Darkness at Noon* (New York: Macmillan, 1941), p. 157.
2. Paul S. Minear, "My Peace I Give to You," in R.H. Stone, ed., *Reformed Faith and Politics* (Washington, DC: University Press, 1983), pp. 31–48.
3. For a modern situation that corresponds roughly to the dilemmas of John's readers, cf. the description of a crisis in the life of Martin Luther King Jr., in Stephen B. Oates, *Let the Trumpet Sound* (New York: Harper & Row, 1982), pp. 87–89.
4. Paul S. Minear, "False Prophecy and Hypocrisy in the Gospel of Matthew," in J. Gnilka, ed., *Neues Testament und Kirche* (Freiburg: Herder, 1974), pp. 79–86.
5. D. Bruce Woll, "The Departure of 'The Way': The First Farewell Discourse in the Gospel of John," *Journal of Biblical Literature* 99 (1980):225–39.
6. George B. Caird, *The Language and Imagery of the Bible* (Philadelphia: Westminster Press, 1980), p. 105.
7. Ibid., p. 51.
8. Woll, op. cit., p. 237.
9. Ibid., p. 238.
10. Boring, op. cit., p. 70.
11. Ibid., p. 223.
12. Feodor Dostoevsky, *The Brothers Karamazov* (New York: Random House, Modern Library, n.d.), pp. 299f.
13. B. Olsson, *Structure and Meaning in the Fourth Gospel* (Lund: Gleerup, 1974), pp. 27f., 138–47.

Chapter VII. When You Have Lifted Up the Son of Man . . .
1. Exodus R. on Psalm 78:20, quoted in T.F. Glasson, *Moses in the Fourth Gospel* (London: SCM Press, 1963), p. 54.
2. Origen, on Exodus 11:2, quoted in J. Crehan, *The Theology of St. John* (New York: Sheed & Ward, 1965), p. 127.
3. In the following paragraphs I have used material from my essay

"Diversity and Unity: A Johannine Case-Study," in H. Weder and U. Luz, eds., *Die Mitte des Neues Testaments* (Göttingen: Vandenhoeck & Ruprecht, 1983), pp. 162–75.

4. Rudolf Bultmann, *The Gospel of John* (Philadelphia: Westminster Press, 1971), p. 679; Raymond E. Brown, *The Gospel According to John* (New York: Doubleday, 1970), 2:936; C.K. Barrett, *The Gospel According to St. John* (Philadelphia: Westminster Press, 1978), p. 118.

5. J.R. Michaels, *Catholic Biblical Quarterly* 29 (1967):102–9.

6. Brown, op. cit., 2:807.

7. Ibid., 2:939.

8. H.A.C. Macgregor, *The Gospel of John* (New York: Doubleday, Doran & Co., 1929), p. 353; D.W. Wead, *Literary Devices in John's Gospel* (Basel: Friedrich Reinhardt, 1970), pp. 55–59; Brown, op. cit., 2:960.

9. E.D. Freed, *New Testament Studies,* 29 (1983) 69. For the most thorough defense of this option, see G. Reim, *Alttestamentliche Hintergrund des Johannesevangelium* (New York: Cambridge University Press, 1974), pp. 51ff., 90, 176.

10. C.H. Dodd, *The Interpretation of the Fourth Gospel* (New York: Cambridge University Press, 1953), pp. 233f., 424f.

11. Bultmann, op. cit., p. 678.

12. G. Richter, *Studien zum Johannesevangelium* (Regensburg: Verlag Friedrich Pustet, 1977), pp. 120–42.

13. Barrett, op. cit., p. 557.

14. Reim, op. cit., pp. 62–70.

15. Other symbolic connotations of water may be found in John. It is used for baptism as well as for purification (1:26; 2:7–9) and for washing the feet (13:1–20). Perhaps the text with the closest affinities to chap. 7 and chap. 19 is the saying of Jesus to the Samaritan: "The water I shall give him will become in him a spring of water welling up to eternal life [4:14]."

16. In this passage it is important to realize that John identifies "the world" for which Jesus gives his flesh, with "the Jews"; in this chapter that controversy reaches a point of great intensity.

17. A fuller exposition of this theme in chapter 6 appears under the title "Homiletical Resources" in *Quarterly Review,* June 1985.

18. Walther Eichrodt, *Theology of the Old Testament* (Philadelphia: Westminster Press, 1967), 2:508, n. 1.

Chapter VIII. Ask and You Will Receive

1. Robert Alter, *The Art of Biblical Narrative* (New York: Basic Books, 1981), p. 179.

2. Cf. Paul S. Minear, *Commands of Christ* (Nashville: Abingdon Press, 1972), pp. 113–31; also "To Ask and To Receive," in D.Y. Hadidian, ed.,

Intergerini Parietis Septum (Pittsburgh: Pickwick Press, 1981), pp. 227–50.

3. "The prophetic vision is many-levelled, mingling past or present with future, the temporal and the eternal, the literal and the metaphorical, history with symbol. . . . In the Fourth Gospel there are no parables because the whole gospel is a parable [G. Vann, *The Eagle's Word* (London: Collins, 1961), p. 12]."

4. M. Eugene Boring, *Sayings of the Risen Jesus* (New York: Cambridge University Press, 1982), pp. 132f., 271, nn. 21–27; Marinus de Jonge, *Jesus: Stranger from Heaven and Son of God* (Missoula, MT: Scholars Press, 1977), p. 163, n. 3.

5. The reference to the *words* of Jesus is easily reduced in its range of meaning. What is in view is "not merely the teaching of Jesus nor the words of Jesus, but the very person of Jesus as manifestation of the Father . . . [which] is not complete until he lays down his life for men [J.T. Forestell, *The Lord of the Cross* (Rome: Biblical Institute, 1974), p. 192]"; also below, chap. IX.

6. Probably the best recent description of the role of the prophets is to be found in Boring, op. cit., pp. 58–136.

7. Perhaps the best way to embrace all these forms of asking is to use the term abiding, with its full Johannine resonance. Cf. Raymond E. Brown, *The Gospel According to John* (New York: Doubleday, 1970), 1:510ff.

8. Gerd Theissen provides a more neutral definition of the continuing interdependence of the risen Lord and his visible representatives. The relation of the wandering charismatics to the bearer of revelation "was characterized by reciprocal expectations. The various christologies express the attitudes of expectation directed toward the bearer of revelation, the ethical and religious commandments formulated what he expected of believers. Mutually determined roles are assigned to both [*The Sociology of Early Palestinian Christianity*, trans. John Bowden (Philadelphia: Fortress Press, 1978, p. 26]."

9. Cf. Jonathan Edwards, *Concerning the End for Which God Created the World*, in *The Works of Jonathan Edwards* (New York: Carter, 1864), 2:chap. 2; Paul Ramsey, *Elements in Jonathan Edwards' Ethics*, American Theological Society, April 7, 1984, pp. 9, 14, 28ff.

Chapter IX. If You Abide in My Word . . .

1. From "A Word," *The Collected Poems of Emily Dickinson* (New York: Crown Publishers, 1982), p. 23. Used by permission of Crown Publishers, Inc.

2. George B. Caird, *The Language and Imagery of the Bible* (Philadelphia: Westminster Press, 1980), p. 47.

3. Northrop Frye, *The Great Code* (New York: Harcourt Brace Jovanovich, 1982), pp. 17, 76.

4. Cf. S. Pancaro, *The Law in the Fourth Gospel* (Leiden: Brill, 1974), p. 2; also, T. Preiss, *Life in Christ* (London: SCM Press, 1952), pp. 19–29.

5. Caird, op. cit., p. 55.

6. C.K. Barrett agrees in the appraisal of the importance of this paragraph as "a theological conclusion and summary of the ministry as a whole. This paragraph corresponds to the Prologue and is of scarcely less significance [*The Gospel According to St. John* (Philadelphia: Westminster Press, 1978), p. 14]."

7. It is a common tendency among contemporary Johannine scholars to deny the Johannine authorship of the Prologue because of supposed contrasts between it and the rest of the Gospel. The Prologue is a hymn that may even have come from another religion entirely. Cf. R. Schnackenburg, *The Gospel According to St. John* (New York: Herder, 1968), 1:224–49; Raymond E. Brown, *The Gospel According to John* (New York: Doubleday, 1970), 1:518–24. I have tried to counter this tendency in an essay, "Logos Ecclesiology in John's Gospel," in Robert F. Berkey and Sarah A. Edwards, *Christological Perspectives* (New York: The Pilgrim Press, 1982), pp. 95–111. I have drawn much of the material in this chapter from that essay.

Chapter X. No One Comes to the Father, but by Me

1. Paul Ramsey, unpublished essay.

2. D. Bruce Woll establishes the fact that 13:31—14:31 is a distinct literary unit, to be interpreted as a whole ("The Departure of 'The Way': The First Farewell Discourse in the Gospel of John," *Journal of Biblical Literature* 99 (1980):225ff.

3. B. Olsson, *Structure and Meaning in the Fourth Gospel* (Lund: Gleerup, 1974), p. 220.

4. M. Eugene Boring, *Sayings of the Risen Jesus* (New York: Cambridge University Press, 1982), pp. 129; 271, n. 16.

5. Olsson, op. cit., p. 196.

6. C.K. Barrett, *The Gospel According to St. John* (Philadelphia: Westminster Press, 1978), p. 454.

Chapter XI. I Am the Resurrection

1. Amos N. Wilder, *The Language of the Gospel* (New York: Harper & Row, 1964), p. 130.

2. George Orwell, *1984* (New York: New American Library, 1961), pp. 24f., 87, 147, 202; also my essay "1984," in Yale Divinity School *Reflection*, March 1984. For discussion of John's use of the idiom of light/darkness, cf. D.W. Wead, *Literary Devices in John's Gospel* (Basel: Friedrich Reinhardt, 1970), pp. 66f.

3. I have noted earlier the use of the "I-Am" formula as indicative of prophetic speech by Christian prophets relaying the word of the risen Christ, in which the whole story of Jesus is viewed in retrospect (Revelation 1:17—3:22; M. Eugene Boring, *Sayings of the Risen Jesus* [New York: Cambridge University Press, 1982], p. 128). The discourse on the *way* in chapter 14 involved the disciples as potential martyrs; the discourse on the resurrection in chapter 11 involved all believers in the dangers faced by Lazarus (12:10).

4. Northrop Frye, *The Great Code* (New York: Harcourt Brace Jovanovich, 1982), pp. 72–73. Cf. also my essay "Some Pauline Thoughts on Dying," in D.Y. Hadidian, ed., *From Faith to Faith* (Pittsburgh: Pickwick Press, 1979), pp. 91–106.

5. Cp. Testament of Gad 4; "As love would make the dead alive, hatred would slay the living."

6. There is a subtle truth as well as ribald humor in the quip "Work for the Lord. The pay isn't great, but the retirement plan is out of this world."

Chapter XII. Where I Am, There Shall My Servant Be

1. Dietrich Bonhoeffer, *Letters and Papers from Prison* (London: SCM Press, 1953), p. 175.

2. David E. Aune, *The Cultic Setting of Realized Eschatology in Early Christianity* (Leiden: Brill,1972), p. 79.

3. B. Olsson, *Structure and Meaning in the Fourth Gospel* (Lund: Gleerup, 1974), pp. 139ff.

4. George B. Caird, *The Language and Imagery of the Bible* (Philadelphia: Westminster Press, 1980), p. 47.

5. Paul S. Minear, "Holy People, Holy Land, Holy City," *Interpretation* 37 (1983):18–31.

6. I have published an extensive analysis of this episode, from which I have drawn some of the following paragraphs: "We Don't Know Where . . . ," *Interpretation* 30 (1976):125–39.

7. C.K. Barrett, *The Gospel According to St. John* (Philadelphia: Westminster Press, 1978), p. 68; Olsson, op. cit., p. 196.

Chapter XIII. I Have Given Them the Glory

1. Frederick W. Faber, "God's Glory Is a Wondrous Thing," *Pilgrim Hymnal* (New York: The Pilgrim Press), 369.

2. Much of the material in this chapter is drawn from my essay "Evangelism, Ecumenism and John 17," in *Theology Today* 35 (1978):5–13.

3. A thorough analysis of the literary structure of this whole chapter may be found in E. Malatesta, "The Literary Structure of John 17," in

Biblica 52 (1971):190–214; cf. J.F. Randall, "The Theme of Unity in John 17:20–23," in *Ephemerides Theologicae Lovanienses* 41 (1965):373–94.

4. A book-length study of this oneness may be found in M.L. Appold, *The Oneness Motif in the Fourth Gospel* (Tübingen: J.C.B. Mohr [Paul Siebeck], 1976), pp. 157ff.

5. An excellent summary of the wide range of interpretations of this prayer may be found in Randall, op. cit., pp. 373f.

6. Cf. H. Sasse, essay on *kosmos*, in G. Kittel, *Theological Dictionary of the New Testament*, 3:894.

7. Ibid.

8. Professor Randall stresses the degree to which this petition is "perfectly in tune with the main themes of the Fourth Gospel: the primacy of the Father . . . the Father's love for the world; his oneness with his Son; and the association of the disciples to this union for the continued glorification of the Father, and for the continued bringing of his love to the world [op. cit., p. 393]."

9. George B. Caird, *The Language and Imagery of the Bible* (Philadelphia: Westminster Press, 1980), pp. 74f.

10. M.R. Miles, in "The Recovery of Asceticism," *Commonweal* 110 (Jan. 28, 1983):41.

Chapter XIV. Look! This Is Your Mother!

1. Paul Ricoeur, *The Symbolism of Evil* (Boston: Beacon Press, 1967), p. 351.

2. I. de Potterie, "Das Wort Jesu 'Siehe deine Mutter' und die Annahme der Mutter durch den Juenger," in J. Gnilka, ed., *Neues Testament und Kirche* (Freiburg: Herder, 1974), p. 213.

3. Ibid., p. 192.

4. Raymond E. Brown, *The Gospel According to John* (New York: Doubleday, 1970), vol. 1, pp. 101–10.

5. B. Olsson, *Structure and Meaning in the Fourth Gospel* (Lund: Gleerup, 1974), p. 112.

6. It is significant that this verb *lambano* is the same verb as that used in 1:11, where the reference is to the acceptance of the Messiah by the messianic people. Cf. also de Potterie, op. cit., p. 216.

7. Paul S. Minear, "The Beloved Disciple in the Gospel of John," *Novum Testamentum* 19 (1977):105–23.

8. De Potterie successfully challenges the current translation, "the disciple took her to his own home." *Home* is not the best rendering of *ta idia*. Those words rather suggest the sheep for whom this shepherd was responsible (op. cit., pp. 208f.).

9. Marinus de Jonge, *Jesus: Stranger from Heaven and Son of God* (Missoula, MT: Scholars Press, 1977), p. 4.

10. Northrop Frye, *The Great Code* (New York: Harcourt Brace Jovanovich, 1982), pp. 140f.

11. Cf. the essay cited in n. 7, above. Should there be this symbolic association of the mother with Rachel and the beloved disciple with Benjamin, it would strengthen the obligations of the Johannine community to carry on the mission to Israel.

12. Ivan Karamazov, in Feodor Dostoevsky, *The Brothers Karamazov* (New York: Random House, Modern Library, n.d.), p. 304.

Chapter XV. Feed My Sheep

1. Archbishop Oscar Romero, San Salvador, shortly before his assassination while celebrating Mass in the cathedral.

2. A Declaration of Korean Christians, in W. Dong, ed., *Korean-American Relations at Crossroads* (San Francisco: Liberty Press, 1982), p. 183.

3. C.K. Barrett, *The Gospel According to St. John* (Philadelphia: Westminster Press, 1978), p. 76.

4. In the words "these are written that you may believe" most scholars have decided that the words "these are written" apply to the whole Gospel, from chapter 1 on, and that we therefore have in these verses a summary of the purposes of the narrator and the original ending of the Gospel, making the next chapter an appendix, probably contributed by another author. I have given a minority opinion on this matter in "The Original Functions of John 21," *Journal of Biblical Literature* 102 (1983):85ff.

5. "The capture of the 153 fish, and the patient apostolic care of the sheep and the lambs, form the climax of the Gospel, not the faith of Thomas [E. Hoskyns, *The Fourth Gospel* (London: Faber & Faber, 1947), p. 550]."

6. See note 4, above.

7. R.H. Strachan supports the view that when Peter returned to his fishing it was as one who did not yet believe in the resurrection (*The Fourth Gospel* [London: SCM Press, 1951], pp. 325, 335).

8. R. Alan Culpepper, *The Johannine School* (Ann Arbor: University Microfilms, 1974), p. iv.

9. It is when interpreters suppose that chapter 21 is primarily concerned to give another account of the resurrection, with an implicit call to believe in Christ, that this chapter appears to be an unnecessary addition to a Gospel that would be complete without it. But it is different once we recognize the interest of chapter 21 in the specific assign-

ments Jesus gave to these two disciples, in the development of their mission, in the different kinds of death, in the distinctive thrust of Jesus' final message, and in making explicit the chain of communication that linked John's readers to the source of revelation. And, as we have seen, apart from this chapter many of the prophetic disclosures in the early chapters would remain unfulfilled. The chapter was designed to help readers make the shift from the faith of the first believers to their own faith, grounded as it is in a different range of evidence, when both of the key shepherds had died.